Icarus World Issues Series

Good Sports
Fair Play and Foul

Series Editors, Roger Rosen and Patra McSharry

THE ROSEN PUBLISHING GROUP, INC.
NEW YORK

Published in 1992 by The Rosen Publishing Group, Inc.
29 E. 21st Street, New York, NY 10010

Copyright © 1992 by The Rosen Publishing Group, Inc.

"**The Ritual Life of Sports**" copyright © 1992 by The Native Land Foundation. Excerpted with permission from the book by Jamake Highwater, *Athletes of the Gods: The Ritual Life of Sports*, to be published by Grove Press in 1994.
"**Playing the Rain Gods**" copyright © 1986 by Miguel León-Portilla. First published in *Historia-16*, no. 117, Madrid.
"**Lice Racing**" copyright © by Aziz Nesin. From the book *Rifat Bey Neden Kashiniyor*, published by Tekin Yayinevi, Istanbul. Translation copyright © 1992 by Joseph and Viola Jacobson.
"**The Socialist Sports Program**" is excerpted from the book *Doping Dokumente: Von der Forschung zum Betrug* by Brigitte Berendonk, copyright © 1991 by Springer-Verlag Heidelberg-Berlin.
"**In the Plaza de Toro**" copyright © 1992 by Peter Müller Peter. Photographs first appeared in the book *España por Dentro*, published by Lancero 123, S.L., Madrid, copyright © 1991 by Peter Müller Peter.
"**The Sunday Races**" copyright © 1992 by Michael Collins. Excerpted from the book *The Man Who Dreamt of Lobsters*, to be published in March 1993 by Random House, a division of Random House, Inc.

All rights reserved. No part of this book may be reproduced in any form without permission in writing from the publisher, except by a reviewer.

First Edition

Library of Congress Cataloging-in Publication Data

Good sports : fair play and foul. —1st ed.
   p. cm. — (Icarus world issues series)
  Edited by Roger Rosen and Patra McSharry.
  Includes bibliographical references and index.
  ISBN 0-8239-1378-3 (hardcover)
  ISBN 0-8239-1379-1 (paperback)
  1. Sports—Juvenile literature. 2. Sportsmanship—Juvenile fiction. I. Rosen, Roger. II. McSharry, Patra. III. Series.
GV707.G55   1992   92-26967
796—dc20   CIP
                                       A

Manufactured in the United States of America

Table of Contents

Introduction — v

The Sunday Races — 1
Fiction by Michael Collins

The Boys of Sumo — 17
Nonfiction by Julie Scherer

Illogical Loyalties — 39
Nonfiction by Filip Bondy

The Ritual Life of Sports — 51
Nonfiction by Jamake Highwater

Running Backs and Running Dogs — 75
Nonfiction by John Krich

Lice Racing — 95
Fiction by Aziz Nesin

In the Plaza de Toro — 109
Nonfiction by Peter Müller Peter

The Socialist Sports Program — 121
Nonfiction by Brigitte Berendonk

Playing the Rain Gods — 141
Nonfiction by Miguel León Portilla

La Máscara! La Máscara! — 155
Nonfiction by Andrew Coe

Glossary — 165

Bibliography — 167

Index — 169

Introduction

"As flies to wanton boys, are we to the gods;/They kill us for their sport." Certainly this is a grim notion of play, but then Shakespeare's Duke of Gloucester was sorely tried, a bloody participant in the high contact sport that is *King Lear*. While the rulebook of the gods may never come to be revealed to us, we mortals have created innumerable games and contests of our own, endeavors in which action can proceed only within very precisely circumscribed parameters. Perhaps to perform within such a gloriously knowable world is our great consolation. After all, whatever transpires will do so over just so much time—usually readily ascertainable by large digitized numerals sans skeleton, sans scythe. Add to this fact that there will be winners and losers, that there's a good chance a foul will be called a foul, and you've got yourselves some happy campers because the ambiguity of our daily life is removed. Sure, we play to win, but we also play for precise definition.

And what does all this have to do with the crack of a good clean single to right, or a halfback's high-stepping to glory at third and ten, or a top-spin backhand lob that hits the back of the baseline and jumps crooked, high and impossible? Those who are knowing might say that all this stuff about the gods and rules and time and space was written by someone who's never played the game. Lest you open this eighth volume of *Icarus* with such a gloomy thought, let me assure you that we approach the world of sports both as lovers and sexologists, both as those fascinated by its ritualistic intermediary powers and as those for whom the sweat of exertion and the quickened heartbeat of the play is the stuff of life itself.

Introduction

In his essay "The Ritual Life of Sports," Jamake Highwater writes, "Sports are one of the most vivid reflections of that persistent upheaval of our vision of ourselves and our world. We *are* the sports we play." Beautifully put, and that reflection of ourselves is not only our thirst for the transcendent through harmonious movement nor our courtship of grace through the artistry of expertise. It is also our sordid, brutish, tacky selves; the ones that dope young athletes on steroids to shore up the prestige of a bankrupt ideology ("The Socialist Sports Program"), the ones that make a sadistic coach push an injured athlete to race against all reason ("The Sunday Races"), the ones that put business before honor and loyalty, perverting human pleasure into profit ("Illogical Loyalties"). Yes, we are the sports we play. We are the way we play them.

Roger Rosen, Editor

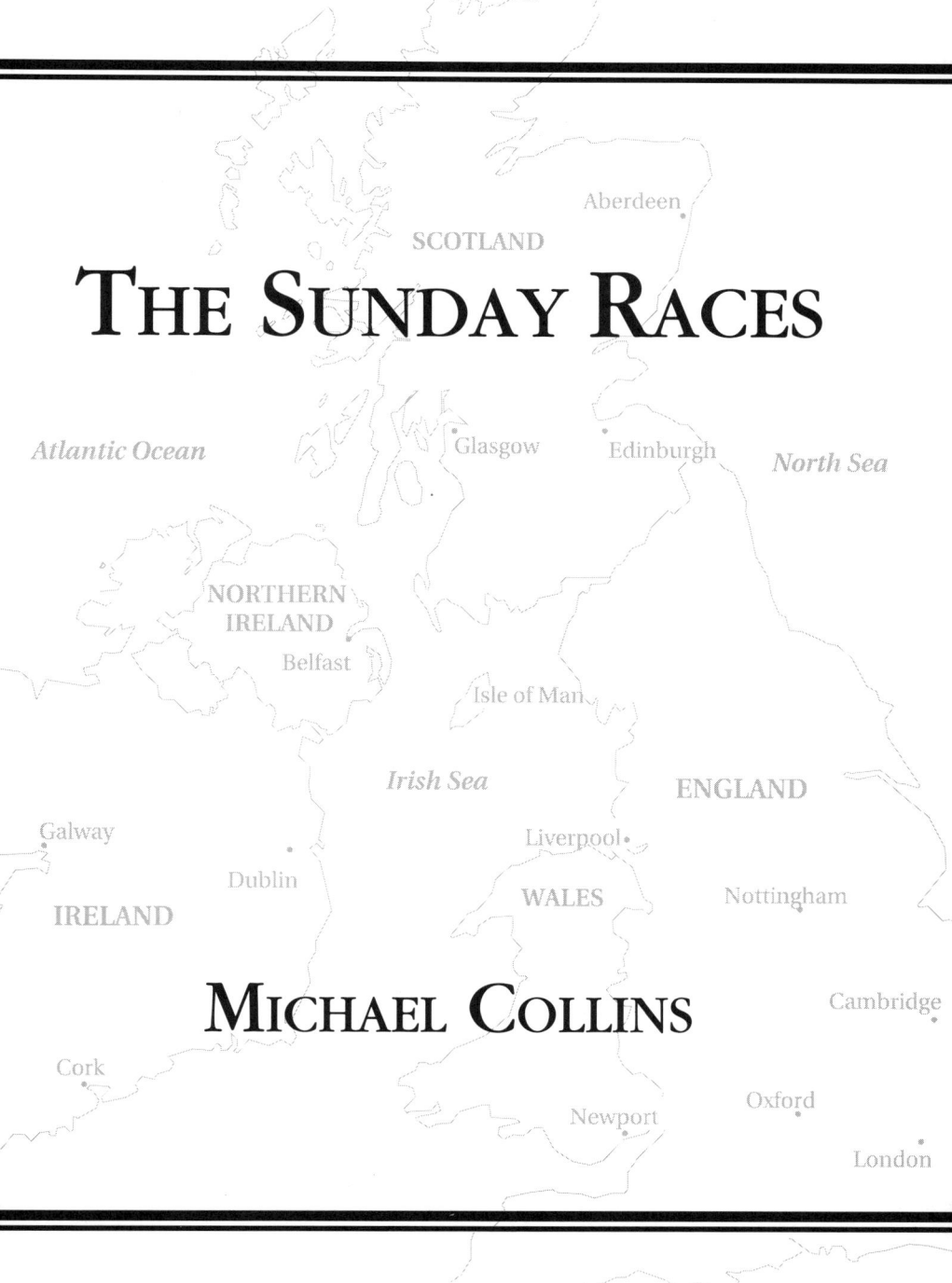

THE SUNDAY RACES

MICHAEL COLLINS

Michael Collins was born in Limerick, Ireland, in 1964. He received a B.A. and an M.A. from the University of Notre Dame. He is currently pursuing a Ph.D. at the University of Illinois, Chicago.

Mr. Collins has traveled internationally as a cross-country runner. He represented Ireland at the International Preparatory School Invitational. After winning a scholarship to Notre Dame, he qualified as an All-American in cross-country and made the First Team All-American.

Mr. Collins's work has appeared in the *Chicago Review* and *Other Voices*, as well as in *Six Irish Writers*, a collection of work by contemporary Irish writers. In 1988 he won the Young Writer of the Year Award and in 1992 was nominated for the Best Fiction in Ireland Aer Lingus Award and for the Best Fiction in Ireland Guinness/Pent Award. The following piece is excerpted from Mr. Collins's forthcoming collection of short stories, *The Man Who Dreamt of Lobsters*, to be published in March 1993 by Random House.

Mr. Collins and his wife, Heidi, live in Chicago.

The Sunday Races

The Sunday morning was silent as always. Emmett hadn't slept well. In his dreams he was moving in slow motion, faces passed him, the earth swallowed him, the dream opening like a wound in his head.

Emmett awoke in his track suit with his running magazines scattered around his bed. He'd fallen asleep reading an article about a tribe of Kenyan runners. The room was cold, the wallpaper teeming with moisture from the dampness. Tentatively, Emmett tensed his injured left leg. It was locked with stiffness, numbed from the bandage tourniquet. He grimaced. The dull numbness throbbed under the covers. He uncoiled the bandage, exposing the thin whiteness of his leg, the black hairs matted with sweat. The unseen muscle tear was getting worse, bleeding invisibly. He put his face in the pillow.

Emmett sat up again in the cold half-light of his room. The space was small, encumbered by a bed that occupied half the room. He let his fingers run over his legs, feeling his ankles, the soreness in the joints. He'd become accustomed to the pain and the injuries. It was part of the game. There were some lads who were on a hundred twenty miles a week. Emmett was grinding on ninety, but he was the best. His pelvis and kidneys took the worst of it. For over a month he'd been passing blood in his urine. He'd heard that was normal at those miles.

It was on the long run that he did the damage, or at least that was what he reckoned. He took a knock against a wall. It wasn't anything at all, yet the constant attrition of the miles compounded the hit. In cross-country running there was never anything sudden like the snapped tendons of sprinters or footballers. The injuries always started as nagging pains, indistinguishable from the usual soreness. A day off and common sense would have been medicine enough, but nothing ever seemed that serious until the morning, when the injury had pooled with blood and swelled over time.

Emmett's thigh was badly torn. He touched the muscle, and a knifing pain ran to his pelvis. He took three aspirin from a bottle on his table dresser, worked up a spit in his mouth, and swallowed. He tasted the acrid powder of the tablets in the back of his throat. He took a bottle of menthol rub from his bag and let his leg rest on the dirty sheets. The bottle had a spongy applicator on a wire. He swabbed the muscle in easy strokes. The odor wafted under his nose as the clear liquid trickled down to the tender skin at the back of the knee. The skin stung and turned pink. Emmett worked his fingers up and down his thigh, letting his thumb bury itself in the unseen injury. The locked stiffness softened, almost acquiescing.

Emmett's feet stuck to the freezing stone in the kitchen as he made the tea. The mugs huddled in the cupboard, and the sugar sat hardened by the morning dampness. He set a tray and went upstatirs. The silence of the morning blanketed his father's face. His father was getting old. Emmett could see the scalp under the hair. "What's that smell?" He squinted his face, "Jasus, what is it?"

"Just some rub for my legs to get dem warmed up," Emmett said as he set the tray down at his father's hips. He could see the outline of his father's thin legs under the covers.

His father scowled, making slurping sounds, coughing.

On the small dresser, Emmett looked at the gray fingers of ash on a saucer. "Yer not supposed to be smokin, Da."

"Are you limpin?" his father asked.

"No...You know, stiff...Dat's all."

His father coughed violently and spilt his tea, leaning forward. "Take...take dis..." The cup of tea toppled over.

"Da..." Emmett took the tray away. He went into the

The Sunday Races

back room where his mother lay sleeping. She had migrated into the spare room to get away from the coughing. Emmett kissed her on the forehead. "I'm off," he whispered.

"You're limpin," Emmett's father said again when he came into the room. "Did you see her?"

"Yeh."

"I hear she's got the church blazing with candles for us, and Jasus don't we need it?" His breath was wheezing as he pulled on another cigarette.

Emmett looked at the rain falling in muted static outside the window.

"Good luck, son." His father's words were a whisper of smoke. Emmett heard only the coughing. Phlegm floated in the spilt tea on the tray.

There was a laconic sleepiness to the morning as Emmett met up with Mr. Brennan. A dirty rain littered the night's rubbish. Pipes spluttered and drains gurgled. Emmett was limping noticeably with the bandage he'd wrapped around his leg.

"How's about this for weather?" Brennan grumbled. His breath had the odor of stout. He could see that Emmett had been crying. Unnerved, he nodded his head agitatedly. "Gimme that bag there. Grand."

"Mr. Brennan?" Emmett began.

Brennan eyed Emmett with suspicion. He could see the pronounced limp in Emmett's walk. "We better head off," he began in a preemptive tone, handling Emmett.

"It's my leg," Emmett look into Brennan's eyes. "I don't think..."

"Relax, will you. There's nothing that a good rub won't get you through. Do you hear me?"

"I...I...Mr. Brennan..."

Mr. Brennan turned his eyes in his head. "Hold your horses awhile. You don't have to do anything you don't want to do, right? How many did you get in yesterday?"

"About six, and couple of sprints." Emmett stood abjectly in the rain under the town clock. "Mr. Brennan, I'm tellin you..."

Mr. Brennan nodded his head. "Now this is what we'll do. We'll head out there and see who's about and explain that you've had a bit of an accident, right? We'll say you took a knock this mornin on the roads coming down and see what the judges say. It'll be all right. Sure, they know you've been winning everything." Brennan let his mouth open in a vacuous smile. "But we should make an appearance. OK?" Brennan said it like a priest giving a sermon, letting a smile mask his anger.

Brennan started his car, rubbing his hands together, cursing as usual. Emmett sat silently. He was afraid to touch his leg, tensing and relaxing it to keep the blood flowing. Brennan turned the radio on. The news was the same as always, something sad or terrible from Saturday night. Accidents on the road. Coups in different countries. Everything seemed to happen on Saturdays. Sunday was a day for news, a silent mourning of a dead week, a retrospective when priests and politicians made sense of things. Brennan checked his watch. It was coming up on eight-twenty. "Jasus, we don't want to be stuck listening to Mass for the sick." He laughed in a forceful manner. "Right?"

Emmett didn't smile. His father listened to that Mass on Sundays.

They had to herd the cows out of the field before the race could start. The week's rain had waterlogged the original course in the lowlands. The farmer who gave up the property was in his Wellingtons, driving the cows through a rusty gate. His wife was with him, a plump middle-aged woman past the change of life. The farmer's face was tattooed with the blackness of the unwashed, an ingrained swarthiness. He prodded a stick into the bony shoulders of his animals as the dogs harassed them, cutting between their legs. "What a whore of a day." The farmer moved about in disgust. He was one of those hard-faced men two generations removed from the great potato famine, a descendant of death. He didn't understand things like sports. His time was lost in the constant attention to his animals and his fields.

"You better get back in the car for awhile." Mr. Brennan sighed. "I don't know what the hell is going on." He looked at the farmer. "Do you have a jacks here?"

"Now, hold on there. I thought you were bringing a portable toilet. That's what Brodder Madden told me."

"Yeah, he's not here yet." Mr. Brennan turned toward a ditch.

The farmer rapped on Mr. Brennan's shoulders. "Don't even think about it. I don't want my cows eating your shite!"

The coldness of the morning was clotted with a grayish gauze of threatening clouds. Emmett took a step back. More cows plodded along nervously. Their eyes were huge black lakes, reflecting Emmett's cold face. They had eyelashes that made them peculiarly feminine, almost tender. The distended sacks beneath their hind legs jiggled as they ran. The farmer pushed on, his wife following him in a kind of bovine trot with her buttocks swaying.

Brother Madden drove up in a minibus with his boys. Madden was upwards of 20 stone. The young runners were skeletons beside him. Emmett looked on quietly, aware of his own thinness. Brother Madden's elephantine feet plodded through the mud. He exuded the corpulence of the religious, a man who never missed a meal in his life. He ate at baptisms, at weddings, at funerals.

Emmett could feel Madden's eyes watching him. "You ready then, Emmett?" Madden let his fat hand maraud Emmett's head.

"I don't think I'll..." Emmett looked at Brennan.

"Right as rain," Brennan chimed.

Rain fell in a cold icy sheet, the mountains obscured in low-blown clouds. It had rained like this for nearly four days straight. The constant rhythm of the rain had followed Emmett for days, at night in bed, at school looking out the window, in the car on the way to the field. The sea itself seemed to engulf the land in this dome of grayness, saturating the whole of the country. The February sky carried with it threats of flu and pneumonia and the deathly skulk of earthy dampness. During this dead season animals went unmilked, stuck in cold rains, while others drowned in lowland fields. The old perished in the grip of arthritis or consumption. It was the limbo season, where darkness rained its effulgence, claiming the infirm.

Emmett was aware of a coldness and the rain seeping into him, compounding his injury. His body was stiff from the previous night's unrest. His track suit smelt of last night's sweat. The hot tea of earlier on was somewhere in his intestines, but he was getting cold. He limped toward the cold stony walls. The field was clotted with the prints of animal hooves, the grass churned with mud and cold water. With the loose rain there was no odor or taste to the morning. His body had been numbed to the sensation of life. He kept hoping the race would be canceled. He wasn't sure that Brennan was going to tell Brother Madden anything. Emmett began crying to himself, first in sniffles, and then tears ran down his face. All he needed was a few days' rest to sort the leg out. If only Brennan would tell them as he said he would.

A sudden shower of hail began pelting the small huddle of cars, sending people in a scatter for cover. The race was off for now. Emmett hobbled toward the car as the sky grew almost dark. Brennan turned on the engine and revved the car, blasting the heater. "Jasus!" He opened an egg sandwich and a flask of tea. "Here, take a sup to warm yourself."

The Sunday Races

Emmett was shivering. The car rocked in the cold wind. "You said you would tell them," he began hesitantly.

Brennan chewed his sandwich, holding his tea close to his face.

"I mean it. You don't own me…" Emmett began crying again. He put his head on the dash, sobbing. "You think I don't want to get on the team?"

"Listen here, sunshine." Brennan quivered with firm solemnity. He squeezed Emmett's arm. "You can't always think of yourself, you hear me…I've given up a year of Sundays for you. And I've asked for nothing ever. So don't you give me this business now. Has your father ever come out here?"

"All you have to do is tell them that I got a knock. They know us, Mr. Brennan. They'll believe you. I just need a week ta get over this thing. It's next week that counts. Come on, please." Emmett raised his face from the dash. "Please."

Brennan whispered, "Self-pity is a bad thing. You hear me, Emmett? You get out there today and prove yourself a man. I thought you were the boy with the dreams, and here I have to beg a pup like you to do me a favor."

"It's not like that…" Emmett's face was twisted with redness.

Brennan banged his flask on on the dash. "You got some nerve. Now you listen to me. You're goin to do the man's thing here if I have to kick your arse around that field myself." His voice bordered on a scream, and then he tempered it with a low pant. "Have you any dacency at all?" Two flecks of froth formed at the corners of Brennan's lips.

There was a claustrophobic air about the car. The windows were fogged with rain and words. Emmett was shaking with nervousness. Running for him had always been something simple, something unshared. Before he'd ever met Brennan, he had gone off on those mornings alone. He had lived his dreams all those years, not Brennan's.

Emmett closed his eyes. Those runs had been internal

struggles fought both inside and outside the body, conscious assaults on hidden roads, winding hills, a series of journeys, into mountains alone, into the organs of his body, slow agonizing runs that reckoned with the physical animal lurking beneath his skin, journeys elemental yet anchored to the basis of civilization, to biology, the intake of oxygen, the supremacy of the heart muscle, the sinews of lean flesh, all those things that trapped prehistoric animals but let man live, eat, and reproduce.

Nobody knew his secrets, the long runs that took him on roads untraveled, passing the crumbling ruins of roofless cottages haunted by cows, running along hidden animal trails. These runs bred a kind of mystifying euphoria, a self-containment removed from the company of others, something beyond the vulgarity of medals and trophies. The fifteen-mile run on a Sunday in the off-season, into the mountains in the early hours of the morning, climbing the snaking roads of reeking offal, hearing the secret lives of animals on sloping fields, their bodies lost in mist...He had felt all that, out there, the haggard endurance of a ragged skeleton, the burning sensation of pain slowly uncoiling in his thighs, the controlled torture, bordering on masochism. Running became a drug, an inflicted resolve over the meaninglessness of that which was left behind in sleeping houses along the seafront in Dun Laoghaire and Bray. At the pinnacle of a climb, there was always that moment to stop and look, to take the eyes off the road and look down at the thin ribboned mist of smoke, the electric wires threading the sky. That was when his alienation held its still, immutable beauty. The land had a haunting aura. Visions of other lands were there. He could imagine the misted dawn of Africa unfurling in the sullen majesty of unseen mountains. He shared secret dreams with others. He remembered from his magazines an African saying on some yellow mountain, "Before you can run with the pack, you must first run alone."

The Sunday Races

Emmett felt the coldness. He was conscious of his own country, the ruddy faces, the smallness of the island shrouded in dampness, the fetid odor of animal waste, the dankess of fungus, the earth with its famine-dead and blackened potatoes. The unforgiving infertility of that field out there, stone and mud. If there was kinship with Africa it was there in this famine death, in the underbelly of these unknown fields with forgotten cottages, the hidden past. Famine and blight lurked under the skin of earth. Emmett could almost smell the sodden flesh in those fields out there. He was amidst the dead, the tongueless, earless, eyeless corpses, inchoate memories like mist, whispering, unknown histories disembodied. It was the loneliness of those runs that resurrected the dead in the half-light of his dreams and journeys.

Slowly Emmett looked at Brennan with concealed hatred. His dreams were frozen. They were stuck in the middle of a torrential rain. Sleet fell in muted splats on the windows. The car was whistling in the wind. His teeth gritted. The menthol ointment was cooling on his legs. He kneaded the injury with the palm of his hand.

Mr. Brennan pretended he was asleep, snoring.

Brother Madden materialized from the rain, tapping the window.

Mr. Brennan yawned and rolled down the window. "Yeah?"

"It looks bad." There was an odor of bacon issuing from Madden's mouth. He walked off in the mud, rapping on other cars.

"You see now, you jumped your horses. You'll probably not have to run at all. And what would be the point in letting on to anybody that you had a bad leg? If they knew that, I'd bet Madden would have one of his fellas get you out there. Isn't that right? You know bloody well it is."

Madden waddled about the cars like a crow. Brennan looked at Emmett. Everything had the aura of a black-and-white war documentary. It was a war of waiting, of endless monotony. Emmett squeezed a worm of cream onto his thighs and shivered.

Madden gave a sudden roar, "We're on."

"That's it then." Mr. Brennan wiped a pasty spit from his lips.

People crept from the cars like creatures from the Ark. Rain beaded on every surface. Everything smelt like salt. Sea gulls squawked and hovered overhead. Mr. Brennan gave his patented nod. "Come here and gimme a look at that leg."

Emmett sat at the side of the car, letting Brennan take his leg. "Ah...right there."

Brennan let his fingers trace the muscle from the hip to the knee. "Tell me where it hurts the most."

"Right there, on the inside of the thigh."

Brother Madden spat in the mud. "Is he all right?" His face was rosy and smooth. He had a big duffel bag slung over his shoulder with the singlets for St. Brendan's and the holy water he made his boys drink.

"Are you off to an exorcism, Brother?" Brennan laughed.

Brother Madden smiled.

"Just giving him a rubdown. We had a hard go last Tuesday on the mountains. He's still stiff."

Madden led his boys off toward the field.

"Are you goin to give it a go?" Brennan queried.

Emmett nodded his head. "It feels a little better," he said hesitantly, standing and testing the pressure on his thigh.

"Come on. Do it for your Da."

Emmett felt the insincerity. "Don't..."

Brennan grimaced and nodded. "Come on, look, you're grand. In a half an hour it'll be over, and then you can take your week. Right now, they won't believe you. They'll think you're scared. You don't want a reputation like that, now, do you?"

The Sunday Races

Emmett acquiesced. "Right..." He tried to smile. He started running slowly. The pain knifed him instantly, his leg wobbling. He stopped and looked about him. Everywhere there were runners emerging in packs into the grayness. A megaphone warbled in the distance. One of the coordinators was marking the course with a wheel. The farmer drove his tractor up the back road, carrying bales of hay into the field, roaring his head off. The men were stomping about, rubbing their hands together, spitting, laughing, and coughing. A couple of dog betting men had arrived in a Granada. Mr. Thompson had set up his caravan, and he was selling tea, sandwiches, and curry chips. The morning stood in its own brooding stupor, the sun lost to the day.

Emmett ran in a stiff trot into an adjacent field. As long as he ran from the knees down the pain was abated. His pores opened and began to sweat. There was an earnestness about the morning, the myopic air, the dourness of sobriety. He tested his leg in the soft muck. The pain was excruciating when he pulled it from the mud.

Emmett urinated against the wall, feeling the hot trickle dribbling on his fingers. He pulled his sweats up. His leg was locked with stiffness. He fought the pain and tried to run, the torn muscle trembling. "Come on, come on..." he said over and over to himself. He fell forward into the mud as his leg gave a twinge of pain, his hip giving out.

"Ten minutes!" the speakers sounded.

Emmett couldn't take the pain. He walked to Brennan, his body drenched in mud, his head held downward.

Brennan wheeled Emmett off to the side, his eyes burning with madness. "You bastard. You get out there, you hear me?" His voice quivered on a shout.

"No!" Emmett roared. "I can't even feel my leg. I swear to you."

Brennan cocked his fist and smashed it into Emmett's face. He lunged forward, grabbing Emmett by the throat. "You're bloody well going to do what I tell you, you hear me?" Brennan spat into Emmett's face. "You bastard. Get out there, or make your own bloody way home. Do you think I've nothing better to do than to screw around with the likes of you?" Brennan could sense Emmett's body folding in his grip. He let go of him; Emmett fell to the ground.

The nothingness of the day and the hour was consumed by the dreams of those thousands of miles. Emmett felt the daze of the grayness, the sting in his face. His tongue was stuck in his throat. He was shaking with shock. He could see himself out there, alone with the silent alienation of his dreams, those things born in the coldness of fields.

Madden and Taylor came running over. "What in the name of God?" Madden used his massive bulk, pushing Brennan away from Emmett. "Are you mad?"

Taylor helped Emmett to his feet. "What happened?"

Emmett kept his head down. "Nothing." He hobbled under Madden's arm to his minivan.

"Five minutes." The loudspeaker voice was distorted in the wind.

Madden shook his head in disgust. "Is it your leg?"

Emmett nodded his head.

"I made that bastard what he is!" Brennan roared in the background. "Get your bloody hands off me, Taylor."

Madden laid Emmett out in the back of his van, draping him with a woolen blanket. "You just rest there awhile. I'll speak to the right people." Madden shut the back of the van and ran off toward the start.

A gunshot out in the distance. Emmett was alone in the small compartment of the van. There were faint roars and whistles outside. He closed his eyes. There was safety in the darkness. He could imagine them out there in the field and the rain. He saw them as a blur. The grayness was filled with the unspoken dreams that went back to those early days when he decided to go into the mountains. He could almost see those animal faces, condemned to slaughterhouses, looking outward with sad eyes. The myriad faces of the betting men poured into his head. They were there saying things with their eyes, rubbing the knuckles of their hawthorn sticks in contemplation. They knew a good thing when they saw it. They were crude farmer types who had an affinity for meat. And they said it to your father's face and looked at your mother, fine breeder that she was, a bitch in heat to rear a pup like you. The hoary, knotted, liver-spotted hands of men who had spent a life running fingers over the muscles of dogs and horses, betting men who could scare the shite out of a bookie, and they knew a good bloody thing when they saw one…They knew all the tricks, there now, the smell of poteen rubbed into the legs heats the pinkness of the muscles, sets them on fire. Oh it kills the pain of fatigue, it drugs nicely, a drop is all it takes, and not too bloody much, or you'll be on your arse, drunk as a whore.

"You know, he gets it from his mother's side of the family."

"Is that a fact?"

"It is by Jasus! They were all workhorses."

And in his quiet gaze, Emmett felt the intoxication of sleep falling upon him. He could feel the rhythm of his breath, the cessation of pain in his leg. He would be out there again, next week or next month. And he would be alone, running amidst immortals, feeling the eyes of the famine dead looking at him with hollow faces as the rain poured into the dead earth.

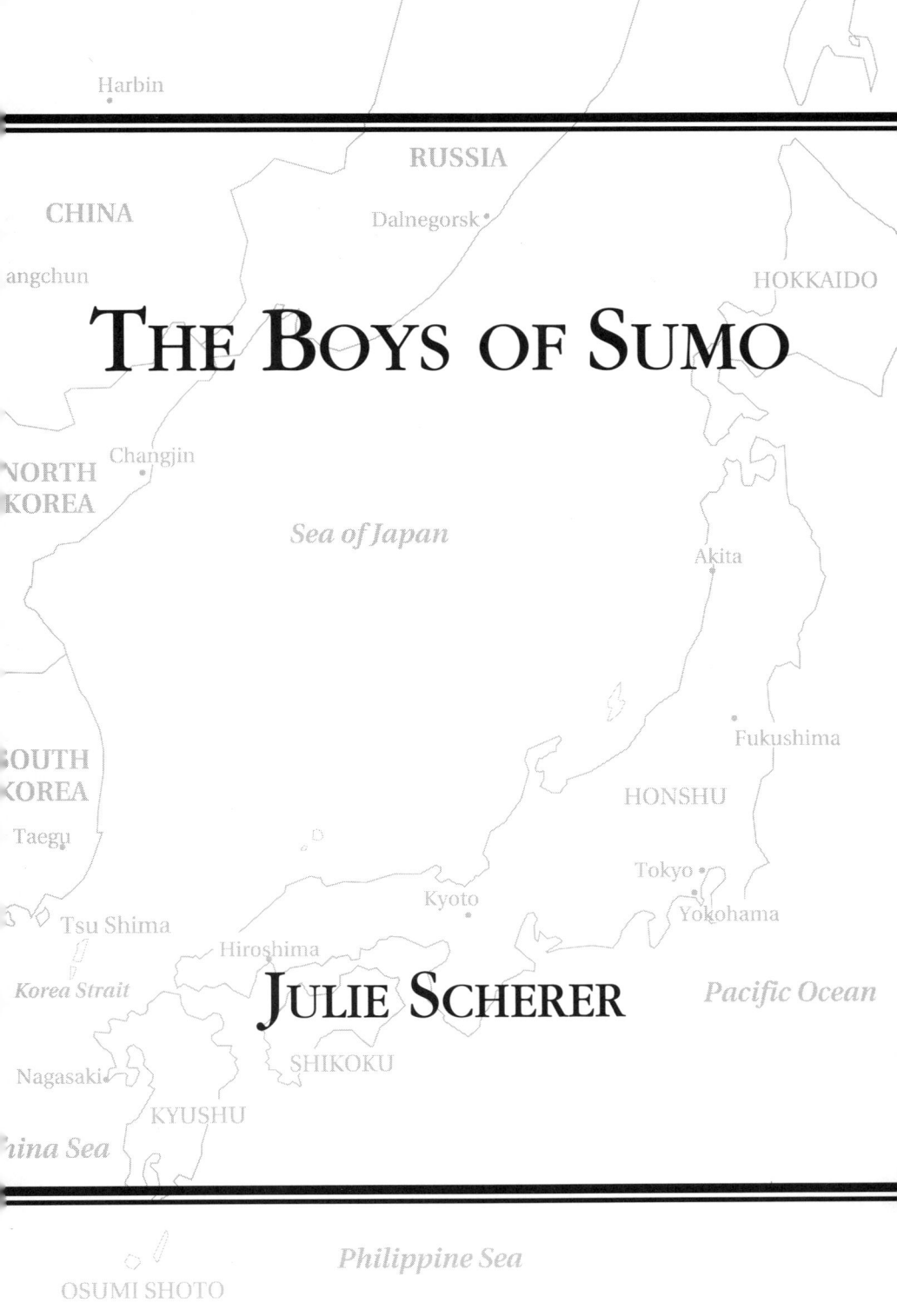

THE BOYS OF SUMO

JULIE SCHERER

Julie Scherer was born in New York City. She studied at New York University, where she received an M.A. in filmmaking. She was a finalist in the American Film Institute Competition for writing, direction, and cinematography for her film "The Way You Look Tonight."

Ms. Scherer studied Japanese in order to work with the prominent Japanese director Masahiro Shinoda. In 1976, she became assistant director to Mr. Shinoda on the production of a documentary on the United States bicentennial celebration. She moved to Tokyo in 1980. Her first three years in Japan were spent producing commercials for the Grey-Daiko Advertising agency. She subsequently branched out into journalism and photojournalism, specializing in coverage of sumo wrestling. Her work was published in the Asahi Newspaper Group newspapers and the Japanese edition of *Sports Illustrated*.

Ms. Scherer's work has been published in the *New York Times*. Her photographs have appeared in *Redbook*, *Sports Illustrated*, and *Travel and Leisure*, among others. For the past three years, she has been an instructor at the School of Visual Arts. The following selection is an excerpt from her work in progress, *The Boys of Sumo*.

Ms. Scherer lives in New York City.

The Boys of Sumo

Sumo is addictive. The smell of the wrestlers' musk hair oil...the rhythm of men soundlessly entering the ring, facing off, crouching, one trying to stare the other down...the sound of wrestlers suddenly leaping forward with tremendous impact of flesh, muscle, bone, and exhaled breath...the sight of skin glistening with sweat...the singing of a winner's name after a match...all remain in your memory. If you go to see sumo often enough, you feel as though it has gotten into your bloodstream. You begin to crave it.

The two written characters for *sumo* mean *mutually* and *to strike*.

SU — Mutually   MO — To Strike

The rules of winning are as simple as the word: either one's opponent leaves the ring, or part of his body other than the soles of his feet touches the ring's surface.

Sumo predates man. Like Jacob's angel, the Japanese gods were skilled wrestlers. According to legend, the warrior god Takemikazuchi secured possession of the Japanese islands by winning a sumo match.

The first recorded human sumo occurred in the fifth century as a religious offering made by an agricultural society. Once a year, in a field or on the grounds of a shrine or palace, two men stripped to their loincloths and pitted all their strength against each other. The contest represented divine power. A sumo victory pleased the gods and was evidence that sacred forces could be harnessed to provide a good harvest. Sumo continued for hundreds of years as part of an annual agricultural celebration.

The period 1482 to 1558 was marked by internecine warfare in Japan. The warrior, or samurai, class was held in high esteem and played an essential role. Each samurai was affiliated with a landowning vassal who had sworn allegiance to a higher lord and so defended territorial integrity of a region from possible invaders. At this time, warriors began to engage in sumo wrestling as a martial art to prove and develop their strength.

In 1615 the Tokugawa clan seized power in Tokyo and subjugated the rest of the country. Regional conflict ceased, and the once crucial samurai became less necessary.

The ensuing period of peace also fostered the birth of a merchant class. Sumo now evolved into an organized form of entertainment, sponsored by the newly wealthy merchants. In Tokyo, Osaka, and Kyoto, sumo houses were established where wrestlers were nurtured and trained. Sumo contests were held several times a year.

The Tokugawa era (1615-1867, known as the *Edo* period, after the former name of Tokyo) saw the development of a rigid class system whose repercussions still echo in modern Japan. From highest to lowest status, the ranks were: *Shi* (samurai), *No* (farmer), *Ko* (artisan), *Sho* (merchant). Priests were above society; at the opposite extreme were those who raised and handled animal products, who were stigmatized as an untouchable group and often considered animals themselves. Ironically, during the *Edo* period, the poorly regarded merchants came to exert a great deal of influence, while the samurai held status without power.

Although skilled in sumo, it is unlikely that many samurai became professional wrestlers. The concept of engaging in popular entertainment affiliated with the mercantile class would have been distasteful. Instead the establishment of commercial sumo became an opportunity—as professional sport has always been—for talented, motivated people from nonprivileged backgrounds to gain money and fame.

Modern sumo reflects characteristics of three social groups: It has sacred elements from its traditional religious origins; a martial aspect from its association with the samurai; and a firm commercial foundation, first developed by *Edo*-era merchants. Accordingly, the *mawashi*, the belt worn by today's sumo men, is not very different from what the holy wrestlers wore in the fifth century. The sumo topknot was introduced by the respected samurai. The existence of sumo as a popular sport divided into forty-three competing stables is a direct result of mercantile support three hundred years ago.

The sumo stable *(heya,* meaning "room" or "house") holds from five to forty active wrestlers, depending on its ability to attract recruits. The stable owner is a retired wrestling star. He lives with the young men. His is the primary responsibility for scouting and training future wrestling talent. If he is married, his wife also lives in the stable, performing a role for the young wrestlers not unlike that of Wendy in relation to the the Lost Boys. She tends them when they're sick or injured, listens to their problems, and encourages them if they are homesick or discouraged. She also orders all supplies for the stable and accompanies her husband to most official sumo events. Attached to the stable but not living in it are sumo judges, hairdressers, additional trainers, and general assistants.

Having developed out of religion, sumo still involves the performance of rights for purification and abolition of evil spirits. The sumo ring is thirteen feet in diameter. It is defined by a thick coil of rope embedded in the ground, which is a substitute for the rice bales that originally marked the wrestling boundaries hundreds of years ago. When a ring is built for an official series of matches, "lucky" objects are blessed and buried under the clay surface by a Shinto priest: soy-flavored rice crackers, seaweed, and dried squid, included for their salt content, to purify; saké as a libation for the gods; and chestnuts, called *kachiguri,* from the root *kachi,* victory. Each time an official round of sumo matches takes place anywhere in Japan, a new ring is constructed and blessed.

When wrestlers prepare to face off against each other, they throw salt into the ring. A wounded wrestler sometimes sprinkles it on his bandages before a match. Sumo conforms with traditions of some Eastern religions by considering females unclean. If so much as a woman's pinkie finger touches the clay of the ring during practice or during an official match, the ring is demolished and rebuilt.

Wrestlers and their stables have always adopted names that evoke strength, good luck, and geographic origin. For example, one of history's first sumo champions was called Inazuma (Lightning). At the end of the 19th century, a champion of the Takasago stable was named Konishiki *(nishiki* means "honor"); the strongest wrestler currently in that stable bears the same name. In the 1950s, a champion from Hokkaido, Japan's northern island, was named Chiyonoyama *(chiyo* is "generation," *yama* is "mountain"). He formed a stable that has traditionally recruited Hokkaido wrestlers. That stable's current owner achieved a record thirty-one championships; his wrestling name was Chiyonofuji *(Fuji* is Japan's most sacred mountain). Other words that are often incorporated into sumo names include: *Taka,* Tall; *Hana,* Flower (with the connotation of "pride and beauty"); *Asahi,* Sunrise; *Shio,* Tide; and *Dai* or *Oh,* Great.

The entrance requirement for recruits is height of at least 5'7" and weight of 165 pounds. The traditional sumo body is heavy, round, and hard, with short, powerful legs. When a wrestler enters the sumo ring, he raises first one leg then another high in place and stamps to rid the battlefield of demons. Opponents then squat opposite each other and extend their arms to show they have no concealed weapons. In these few tense minutes before the wrestlers clash, eye contact between the men is essential. A wrestler is identified as a coward if he can't meet and hold his opponent's gaze. Purists maintain that the match is decided by the intensity of the mutual stare, making the subsequent physical contact almost irrelevant.

In the final moments of preparation, wrestlers go into a crouch, with clenched fists lightly touching the clay in front of them. Bodies are poised to enhance momentum and shock in the instant of attack. Ideally, the wrestlers' breathing rhythm coincides so they are ready to spring toward each other simultaneously at any moment. The ratio of preparation time (two to four minutes) to physical combat (average twelve seconds) produces the effect of a slowly building drama resolved in a brief, spectacular explosion.

My introduction to sumo came in the early 1980s when I was producer at an ad agency in Tokyo. For our detergent product, it was decided to try a warm, humorous approach, starring the sumo wrestler Takamiyama. Jesse (his original name) is Hawaiian, the first foreign-born man to gain a high sumo rank. Forty years old when we began work in 1981, Jesse was still an active wrestler and a TV commercial veteran. His tolerant nature was evidence of having persevered through trials and having overcome barriers.

The strict master/apprentice custom that sumo shares with most traditional Japanese disciplines required that Jesse be accompanied to the set each day by one or two young wrestlers to attend to him. Before beginning the commercials, I had read about sumo and watched it on TV. When work started, I spoke English with Jesse and Japanese with the young wrestlers. We became friends. They invited me to their stable, where I began photographing the wrestlers at practice and official matches.

* * *

For recruits and the lowest-ranking men, sumo practice begins each day at about 6 a.m. The wrestlers do bending and stamping warmup exercises. They take turns slapping a kind of large, wooden pillar that one can find imbedded at all practice areas.

The ideal of sumo wrestling is for a wrestler to be rooted in the clay of the ring. The body's center of gravity must be low, and thighs and calves must be strong and supple to make it impossible for an opponent to unbalance you.

Wrestlers crouch, then shuffle quickly forward, knees slightly bent, without the soles of their feet leaving the dirt. The young men then wrestle in elimination rounds, the strongest getting the most practice. When a man winds down after a hard morning drill, he "borrows the chest" of an opponent: Head down, arms extended forward, the attacker charges a stationary man who gives no resistance other than his weight. The attacker pushes until the opponent, who remains standing, has been pushed so far backward that his heels are up against the thick straw rope of the ring. Then the opponent slaps the attacker's back and pushes him over, causing him to roll. Since even a victorious wrestler is often knocked down by a falling opponent, sumo wrestlers practice tumbling in ways that avoid injury. The attacker charges repeatedly and allows himself to be pushed over each time. Then he reaches a point where he gasps for breath, feeling that he can no longer move. Mud-streaked, groaning, he is dragged or kicked around the ring by his opponent until he is willing to push the absolute limits of his stamina by getting up and charging once more. And then again.

"You learn sumo not with the mind, but with the body," is a saying frequently used by trainers. Most recruits enter sumo between the ages of fourteen and sixteen. A new young wrestler is completely at the mercy of those above him. Sumo rank is achieved not by age, but by strength. The only way to advance is by winning. It is not unusual

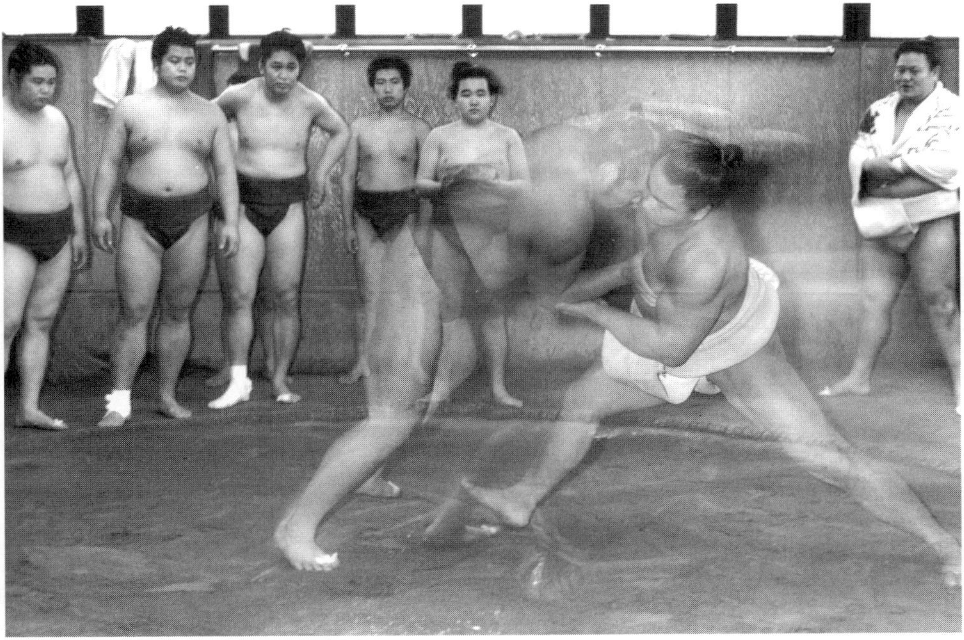

© Julie Scherer

The Yokozuna *"Wolf"* Chiyonofuji *(right foreground) utilizes his speed in practice with a lower-ranking man of his stable.*

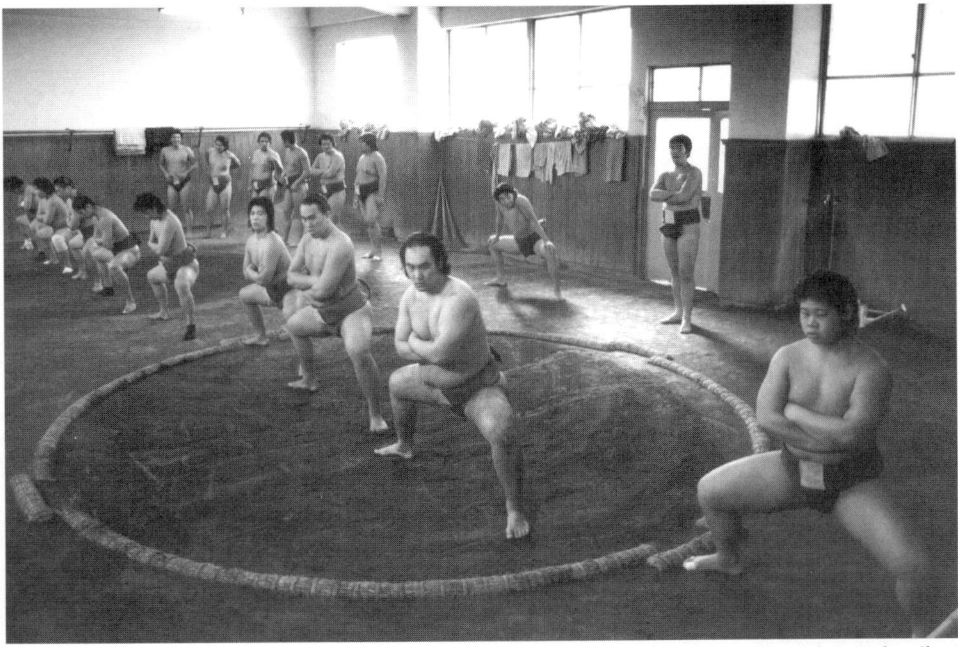

© Julie Scherer

Recruits are taught basic sumo exercises in a practice ring at the Tokyo Kokugikan (National Sport Arena).

for an older wrestler to be the "apprentice" of a younger "master" if the latter has proven greater strength.

At about 9 a.m., the strongest men arrive and start practice. They perform the same warmups as those who precede them. When they wrestle, however, there is a longer "psyching out" period of crouching and staring. During the moments before the charge, sweat is wiped from their bodies by lower-ranking wrestlers. As the larger men repeat the cycle of warming up, wrestling, and winding down, steam visibly rises from their gleaming skin.

One quick way to identify men during practice is by the color of their belts. The lower ranks wear gray; the higher wear white. During official matches, the latter group dazzle with silk belts in all the colors of the spectrum. The belt's function is threefold. It protects modesty, it protects a vulnerable part of the body, and it serves as a weapon for one's opponent. Many of sumo's moves involve grabbing an opponent's belt as a way of unbalancing or pushing him out of the ring.

Typically the two to four hours of morning practice are followed by a bath and grooming of the topknot by the stable hairdresser. Lunch, which is the main meal of the day, is a stew called *chanco*. Variations depend on available ingredients and who is doing the cooking. *Chanco* is a mixture of vegetables and beef, pork, chicken, or seafood. Accompanying it are bowls of rice, salty pickles, and beer. Often, fans attend practice and bring gifts of food. A nap or rest time takes place after eating. The noon meal is designed to provide bulk and sound nutrition. A friend of mine told me how his family prepared him for entrance into a sumo stable: "My dad always used to say, 'Eat until it reaches back there [he indicated his upper back] and up to here [holding his hand at his throat].' Dad thought that was the way to good health. So my mom's cooking...stuck to me."

Exercise, good nutrition, and rest are the basic elements of training for a wrestler. All are necessary for creating the massive, uniquely strong sumo body, one half step above mortal.

After lunch, the lower-ranking men have chores: They do all the cooking, cleaning, and laundry for the members of the stable. When these tasks are completed, afternoon and evening are free time. Many wrestlers use part of the afternoon for weight training. Leisure also means an opportunity to participate in or watch baseball or golf, play video games, and visit friends. Those in the lowest ranks, who have the least money, cook supper at the stable. The higher-ranking men, who have fans in business and politics, are usually taken out for a meal and entertainment. In principle, everyone who lives at the stable has to be back before the stable is locked at about one a.m. (But the highest-ranking men have keys.)

The 250-year-old Sumo Association is the governing body of the sport. It holds in trust 105 names of illustrious wrestlers throughout sumo history. The Association mirrors Japanese society in that it has a provision for lifetime employment for its best wrestlers. When a strong wrestler retires, he has the option of remaining within the Sumo Association. If he has succeeded in gaining a high rank and wealthy fans, he can purchase the right to one of the 105 names and become a sumo "elder." As an elder, depending on the name he has received, he can run his own stable, become a trainer for someone else, or be an administrator for the Sumo Association. The most powerful names cost several hundred thousand dollars. While the Sumo Association welcomes most young men who fulfill the minimum physical requirements, it does not guarantee retirement security for all. A wrestler heading into his mid- and late twenties must carefully evaluate his own potential. If he has not already achieved a high rank, he will serve himself best by leaving sumo and beginning another career. Some men who do quit manage to retain sumo atmosphere by opening restaurants that serve *chanco* stew. The Association, by offering only a limited number of retirement slots, insures that only the strongest, most brilliant, and most determined wrestlers remain in the sport to train future athletes.

Official sumo competitions or rounds take place seven times a year in four major Japanese cities. There are fifteen days of matches in each of the seven rounds. As the matches proceed, men who have been winning are pitted against each other. The wrestler who wins the most matches takes the championship of that round. Most wrestlers never win a championship. Those who do, move up in the ranks and become part of sumo history. The rungs of the sumo ladder are as follows:

Yokozuna = sumo "god"

Sanyaku:
The three highest ranks {
Ozeki = great barrier
Sekiwake = flanking the barrier
Komusubi = lowest of the three ranks

Makuuchi = first "real" rank
Juryo = the amount of salary paid to wrestlers in *Edo* times

Makushita = below rank
San dan me = third level
Jo ni dan = second level
Jo no kuchi = entry level

The Boys of Sumo

The men of the lowest four levels wrestle only seven times during each official round. Those four sumo levels have their own "minor league" championships. The major leagues begin with *Juryo*, the fifth level. From *Juryo* on, a man wrestles every day of the official round. A *Juryo* wrestler is permitted to marry and live outside the stable, but that is a tenuous privilege. With the exception of the top two ranks, an injury or a series of losses can send a man tumbling down the ladder. If a *Juryo* wrestler descends to *Makushita*, he has to move back into the all-male communal sleeping quarters.

The sixth level, *Makuuchi*, contains more than twelve sublevels, each one moving a wrestler closer to *Sanyaku*. At *Ozeki*, the highest point within *Sanyaku*, a wrestler has reached the peak from which he can no longer fall. Even if he cannot advance, he retires with his title and status intact. Reaching *Ozeki* is a tremendous achievement, gained with the ultimate level of skill.

The title of *Yokozuna* goes beyond athletic rank and approaches godhood. At the beginning of each day's sumo, a *Yokozuna* is introduced into the ring wearing a white rope belt. Hanging in a row from the belt *(yoko* means "side by side," *zuna* is "rope") are pieces of white paper folded like those suspended from a Shinto shrine. They represent prayers. When an *Ozeki* is promoted to *Yokozuna*, his first sumo is always performed at the Yasukuni Shrine in Tokyo, a holy site built to honor the Emperor and Japan's war dead. In the history of sumo, only sixty-three men have risen to this height.

In its position as the most traditional of Japanese sports, sumo attracts a wide range of fans. Many of the most loyal remember that sumo wrestlers formed an elite corps of soldiers in World War II. The late Emperor Hirohito was an enthusiastic fan, attending sumo three or four times a year.

Sumo is called a world of "real power." This refers to the fact that sumo wrestlers have only their bodies with which to fight. The bodies may be strengthened by practice and diet. Finally, it is skill and determination that enable a man to triumph.

A nickname for sumo is "the naked world." It is a sexy event to watch. High praise for a wrestler is to say that he has "rice cake skin" meaning his skin is as smooth, glistening, and pale pink as soft rice dough. The opportunity to watch virtually naked men utilize all of their strength in a burst of violent, skilled combat attracts fans of both sexes and all ages.

The first and most festive sumo of each year coincides with the Japanese New Year's holiday in January and takes place in Tokyo. That city also hosts sumo in May and September. The Osaka matches are held in March. In July, the Sumo Association travels to Nagoya; many wrestlers dread this round because of the intense, sticky heat. December matches are held in the southern city of Fukuoka. Since the latter half of the seventeenth century, Tokyo has been sumo's home base.

When the Sumo Association leaves Tokyo for competitions in other cities, each stable lodges in a Buddhist temple or a local inn. That the representatives of an activity based in Shintoism stay in Buddhist temples is evidence of the easy coexistence of these two religions in Japan as well as an affirmation of sumo's religious roots. In temples, the covered altar is pushed to the back of the room and replaced with a TV set so that the men can watch each other on the daily sumo broadcasts. The straw-matted floor becomes a multicolored sea of *futon* each night. Except for those in the highest ranks, everyone sleeps together in the main room. Each stable has not only active and retired wrestlers, but judges and hairdressers traveling with it. A wrestler friend laughed as he told me how when touring, the latter group is at risk for its life. At night when the men come back from parties, a *futon* covering a sleeping wrestler is identifiable because it rises into a hill, but a

Early morning sumo warmup in Ono City, Fukui Prefecture, during the provincial tour.

careless wrestler is very likely to step on and crush a flat, sleeping judge or hairdresser.

On tour, practice almost always takes place outdoors. Fans gather each morning, jockeying for position, bearing children on their shoulders. In Tokyo, the Kokugikan (National Sport Arena) is sold out for at least half of the fifteen-day round of matches. But it is outside Japan's capital that the country most clearly expresses its love of sumo. During the months between official matches, the Sumo Association tours Japan's small towns. Provincial matches are often held in a ring constructed in a school playing field, so that the audience can sit around it on the grass. A local wrestler—preferably a high-ranking one—is specially introduced to the crowds.

These provincial matches are not entered on a man's record. This creates a festive, theatrical mood. On tour, the men can perform *Hanazumo* (*hana* meaning "celebratory" as opposed to competitive wrestling). At a match I attended in Ono, near the Japan Sea, two of the lower-ranked wrestlers engaged in comic sumo. In the real sport before the clash, wrestlers often rinse their mouths; a ladle from a bucket at ringside is filled and handed to them by the winner of the previous bout. It is called "water of strength." That afternoon, the comic wrestlers took ladle after ladle, filled their cheeks, and spat the water out at each other. One man grabbed the other and swung him upside-down, pounding his head into the dirt surface of the ring. *Hanazumo* also includes a demonstration of the hairdresser's art: A wrestler seated himself in the ring's center. Behind him stood a hairdresser, looking very small in comparison. To the accompaniment of an announcer's commentary, the man combed, oiled, pulled, and shaped the wrestler's long black hair. The wrestler then stood and showed the finished sumo topknot to all sides of the ring.

At the same match, an old woman scrambled over to a hometown wrestler who stood below the ring. Her head

The Boys of Sumo

reached only to the middle of his stomach. She put her arms around one of his thighs and hugged tenaciously. Embarrassed, the wrestler had a hard time shaking her off. A local tour is the one chance for a fan actually to touch an idol.

For the two days of this provincial match, Ono's narrow sidewalk hosted groups of tall young wrestlers, blue and white cotton robes pulled sleekly across their stomachs. They had a rolling gait and the dignified level-shouldered posture of athletes and dancers. The men talked, laughed, and nudged each other as they sauntered around town. Some had headphones over their topknots and cassette players tucked into their kimono belts. They strolled in and out of record stores, coffee shops, and bookstores. The streets were filled with the musk smell of their hair oil.

In August, the wrestlers head north, escaping the heat and entering a region famous for producing sumo champions. Conventional wisdom has it that trudging through snow strengthens the legs. Northern Japan is the birthplace of a champion who became sumo's John, Paul, George, and Ringo rolled into one.

His family name is Akimoto; wrestling name, Chiyonofuji. His nickname is "Wolf." His former trainer, in a sumo memoir, tells the story of what it was like when Akimoto joined the stable. Unlike other fifteen-year-olds, he did not seem shy. As the boy's school-length hair grew longer, the trainer was struck by how Akimoto's gaze never flinched from his—the eyes looking out through strands of black hair were bright and piercing. On the night of a full moon, the trainer suddenly knew of what Akimoto reminded him. Calling the boy over, he said, "OK, Wolf! Bay at the moon!" Akimoto shook his hair, threw back his head joyfully, and howled.

By sumo standards, Akimoto was never able to become fat, no matter how much he ate—no matter how long he rested after the day's *chanco*. He had been a running and swimming star in junior high school and was now encouraged to develop his speed. As Chiyonofuji continued in sumo, he became prone to collarbone injuries. Sports doctors suggested that he cover the area with layers of muscle. Through rigorous exercise and weight training, Chiyonofuji became the first highly muscled sumo wrestler. He was often compared to a football player because of his strength and speed. Ten years after joining the stable, Chiyonofuji had climbed his way to the uppermost levels. Japan became locked in the throes of "Wolf Fever." Emerging from the stable, he could get past teenage fans only by wearing dark glasses and a cap to hide his topknot. In 1984, three years after ascending to sumo's top rank, he married the beautiful granddaughter of Fukuoka City's powerful former mayor.

The first time I tried to photograph Wolf, my hands shook. He was sitting on a stool in the sports arena aisle, calmly waiting his turn to ascend the ring for a charity sumo performance. Not long afterward, I visited his stable to photograph morning practice. The lowest-ranking men were in the ring, exercising and squaring off against each other. Sometime between eight and nine o'clock, Wolf entered the room. His face was puffy, not yet awake. Speaking to no one, he began warmup exercises, raising each leg high in place and stamping it down. Gradually, he started to call out gruff admonitions to the young wrestlers. He positioned himself in the middle of the ring, allowing the men to run at him, trying to knock him off balance. As each one rushed forward, Wolf flung, pushed, and slapped him back. If a boy teetered at the edge of the ring, he was pushed again. I noticed that Wolf began to brighten; his face lighted up with a smile. When a boy fell, Wolf ground his foot into crotch and thigh. Walking across the ring, he stepped down again, this time hard on the foot of a prostrate young man. Toward the end of practice,

The Boys of Sumo

Wolf noticed me photographing him. He stood on the back of a fallen wrestler and balanced there with his arms extended. The boy writhed in pain. Wolf look straight into my camera lens, smiled, and shouted, "Ta dah!" as though performing a circus balancing act. In my diary that day I wrote:

> Chiyonofuji burned brighter and brighter. It didn't seem like gratuitous sadism. If there was a chance that one of those boys would become as strong as he, it was more than worth it. Probably Chiyonofuji had submitted to that kind of treatment when he was young. But how could there have been anyone . . . There is no sport, no work in the world that creates something like him. Nothing could have bred Chiyonofuji's skin, shining in the fluorescent morning light of the practice ring, except something in outer space.

This episode was an epiphany, because Wolf was a *Yokozuna.*

Another *Yokozuna* from the north was Asahifuji, who joined sumo out of college at the age of twenty-one. While rising through the ranks, he told me that he felt he succeeded not so much by being strong, but by being "dull ...having 'fat' nerves...I rarely get nervous or tight," he said. Asahifuji had a gentle expression and a soothing, seductive voice. In his early career, with a seemingly unflappable disposition and large, down-turned eyes, he earned the nickname "Sea Slug." Asahifuji's sumo was fluid and intelligent. Perhaps because of his easy-going personality, his reign as an active *Yokozuna* lasted less than two years before he retired—compared with "hungry" Wolf's ten years wrestling as *Yokozuna.*

One of today's most popular young wrestlers is Takahanada. His family is part of sumo tradition. The stable to which he belongs is run by his father, a legendary *Ozeki:*

physically a precursor of Wolf, he never became round, but depended completely on speed, strategy, and muscular strength. Takahanada's uncle, a former *Yokozuna*, was a recent Director of the Sumo Association. Takahanada's older brother is with him in the same stable, but holds a lower rank. Having won the championship last January, Takahanada moved up to sumo's third-highest position. He entered the sport in 1988 and raced up the ladder in less than four years. He is nineteen years old. Takahanada is strong, handsome, and popular without being controversial.

A controversy creating turmoil in the current sumo world involves the high-ranking wrestler, Konishiki, and charges of racism. Jesse Takamiyama, whom I met while working on the TV ad and who now has his own stable, brought Konishiki into sumo in 1982 when the latter was eighteen. Konishiki's ancestry is Samoan; he graduated from high school in Hawaii, where he was a football star. When he first joined the stable, he decorated his area of the communal bedroom with posters of kung-fu star Jackie Chan and stacks of funk and dance music tapes. From the beginning, Konishiki was larger than most of the other wrestlers with whom he lived. He began a high-speed move up in the ranks, gaining sumo's third-highest place in less than two and a half years. He became *Ozeki* at the age of twenty-three. Konishiki has managed to learn Japanese rapidly and well. I know him to be at least as brilliant as his "older brother" Jesse, with a similarly ready sense of humor. Konishiki's discipline and independence remind me of Wolf.

Trouble began with articles appearing in the *Japan Economic Journal* and the *New York Times*. The former newspaper printed its version of a casual exchange between Konishiki, another wrestler, and a reporter. The background of the article was that in March 1992, after winning his second championship as *Ozeki*, Konishiki had not—as many had thought he would—been raised to the *Yokozuna* level by the Sumo Association. Rumors began to fly that Konishiki had accused the Sumo Association of racial prejudice, claiming that the only reason he had not been promoted was because he was not Japanese. Subsequently, the *New York Times* printed its translation of the story, embellished by its reporter's speculation on the depth of conservatism in the Sumo Association.

The Sumo Association demanded an explanation. Konishiki was dispatched to the Association Director by his trainer; an emergency press conference was held. Konishiki denied having ever made a statement about racism. The Director announced that in regard to a promotion, although Konishiki had won the necessary number of championships, he had not won a sufficient total number of matches to satisfy the *Yokozuna* Council's requirements. He said that Konishiki had to be increasingly aware of being in a public position that required him to weigh the dangers of frivolous talk and actions. Last, he wanted everyone to know that he was greatly impressed with Konishiki's strength, hard work, and skill in both the practice and official rings. He hoped that Konishiki would continue to concentrate and become a *Yokozuna* of whom the Association would be proud.

Whether or not he becomes *Yokozuna* in the near future, it is a fact that since Wolf's retirement, Konishiki has been recognized as the strongest wrestler in sumo. He has fulfilled one requirement for becoming *Yokozuna* by having won two championships as *Ozeki*. The other prerequisites are vague. It is ultimately up to the *Yokozuna* Council of the Sumo Association to decide when a wrestler is ready to be appointed a "god."

Since 1986, the last four *Yokozuna* have turned out to be relative disappointments. Because of injury, unbecoming conduct, or failing strength, they have not been able to balance on top of the mountain for long. If the Sumo

Association is acting conservatively this time, perhaps there is a valid reason. Are the managers of the Association racist? Does Konishiki perceive them as such? At the moment, answers lie only in the consciences of those concerned.

Recent events have added ironic footnotes to the "Konishiki Controversy." After Konishiki won the March sumo, the next championship was taken by another non-Japanese wrestler, a Hawaiian. For one of the very rare times in history, there is no *Yokozuna* in sumo—either Japanese or non-Japanese.

Approximately two hundred recruits enter sumo each year. At present, thirty-four non-Japanese men are wrestling at various levels, from lowest place to *Ozeki*. As a percentage of the general population, very few young Japanese men choose a career path involving the disciplined, traditional life of a sumo wrestler. It is unlikely that a significantly large number of Americans, Europeans, Asians, and Africans will join, let alone dominate the sport.

One of the Sumo Association's officials has recently said, "It's not like there is a French or Chinese Sumo Association. If a foreign man wants to become a sumo wrestler he has to come to Japan, live in a stable, undergo the trials of being a new recruit, practice, grow his hair into a topknot, learn Japanese, become strong, skillful, and win matches. If a foreigner is willing to do that, we welcome him."

Sumo is *kokugi* (*koku* is "country," *gi* means "skill"). It is the national skill and it is also the national sport. The traditional sumo expression, "Sumo is learned not with the mind but with the body," is universally understandable to sport participants and fans. Konishiki could echo Magic Johnson's comment, made at 1992 Olympic practice:

"No more questions. No more anything. Let's just play."

Illogical Loyalties

Filip Bondy

Filip Bondy was born in New York City in 1952. He holds a B.S. in Journalism from the University of Wisconsin and an M.A. from the Annenberg School of Communications, University of Pennsylvania.

Mr. Bondy has traveled extensively as a sportswriter and has written for the *New York Daily News*, the *New York Times*, *Sport* magazine, *Sports Illustrated*, the *Village Voice*, and the *Washington Post*. He has received several awards including the Feature and Column Prize of the Professional Basketball Writers Association in both 1988 and 1990, and the Feature Award in the New York State Associated Press Contest. He was nominated for a Pulitzer Prize for a series on race relations within the NBA. Mr. Bondy is the author of *The World Cup* and most recently coauthored the book *The Selling of the Green: The Financial Rise and Moral Decline of the Boston Celtics*.

Mr. Bondy lives in New York with his wife, Lynnell Hancock, and their two children.

Illogical Loyalties

The Cubbies. Now, there was a baseball team. Baby bears bouncing around an ivy-covered stadium in faraway Chicago. Ernie Banks, smiling hero, with happy patches of sky blue on his uniform.

They were a midsummer's daydream, the perfect segue to my autumn passion, the Baltimore Colts. Galloping infant horses, going deep, horseshoes on their helmets, chasing down perfect 40-yard spirals from Johnny Unitas.

These were the soft-focused infatuations of a sports-obsessed kid, still clinging to baby animal images while growing up hard and athletic in the age of booming babies and Bambi. My room was filled with all the trappings of a six-year-old. There was a security blanket. There was a Zorro outfit. There was a stuffed dog. And there were wrinkled felt pennants on the wall, from the Cubs and Colts, the only professional sports teams in America with the sort of nicknames that could sing a child softly to sleep.

My father, who loved Willie Mays, was beside himself. How could his son, growing up in New York City, home of Mickey, Willie, and the Duke, turn his back on such obvious geography? Trips to the Polo Grounds and Yankee Stadium did no good whatsoever. I eyed the out-of-town scoreboard and waited to see if the Cubbies could mount a comeback against the Pirates in Pittsburgh.

The Cubs and Colts were my favorite teams for what I was certain would be eternity. I would catch as many Colt games as I could on television, worshiping at the shrine of that crew-cut, drop-back quarterback, Johnny U. I would wait for effervescent Banks to come into town, then I'd root alone for the Cubs in the stands at the Polo Grounds, popcorn in one hand, glove in the other. Ernie's homer would surely find me in the bleachers, special delivery, from Mr. Cub to Mr. Cub Fan.

Everybody thought I was a lunatic, or else they surely would have wrapped my Cub banner around my prepubescent neck. I didn't care. I would remain loyal, monogamous to one team in each sport, for better or worse, through collapse and contention. Most of my friends did the same, for different teams. By doing so, they formed their own social clubs, with passwords like "Roger Maris" or "Sandy Koufax." A few of my friends switched allegiance at the drop of a pennant race. I thought very little of these spectating butterflies, flitting toward the most glamorous team du jour.

My devotion remained steadfast for many years, even though the rewards were negligible. The Cubs, hopeless dolts since World War II, won absolutely nothing and blew an enormous late-summer lead in that terrible season of 1969. Soon after, the Colts became the first National Football League team to lose the Super Bowl, a disgrace of historic proportions. Unbearably, the most humbling defeats always seemed to come at the hands of New York teams like the Jets or Mets. I was scorned and mocked by my schoolmates, who earned a fortune in quarters from me in a series of demoralizing bets. I felt that, ultimately, my devotion would be rewarded. I was rooting for the good guys, who just needed more time.

Thus burdened, I toted my loyalties into manhood, where I was still certain they would survive. They did not. Today, as a far more cynical observer of sports, I can honestly say I would not wager a used notepad on whether the Colts or Cubs win another game, or even whether they will be eliminated by another nasty conglomerate of New York players.

* * *

Illogical Loyalties

Because I loved pro sports, I became a sportswriter. But because I became a sportswriter, in part, I stopped loving pro sports. Viewed at close range, these athletes were far from model citizens, or interviewees. Reggie Jackson, pinstriped hero, belched in my face. Patrick Ewing leered at my notebook as I approached and would not tell me whether his sprained ankle was improving. Yogi Berra, naked after post-game shower and gulping down greasy chicken wings and meatballs in the manager's office, was more horrific than colorful. He was a villainous Batman caricature come to life. Yogi grunted, he didn't speak. Where were all those homespun malapropisms? I'd known dozens of friends who were much funnier than this.

Sportswriters, once wide-eyed six-year-olds, root only for ourselves. We cheer for the best story that can develop in the shortest time. Deadline pressure forces us to applaud silently, tactfully, for whichever team moves ahead early in any game. If the hated Mets break out to a 4-0 lead over the Cubs, I start writing my early-edition story with the notion that the Mets will win the game. I root hard against the Cubs, my teddy-bear team, because a comeback would render all my work meaningless.

My disaffection, however, reaches beyond these very practical matters. As I matured, my favorite teams were not as central to my existence as they once were. I married. I had two kids, who played in Little League games that were much more exciting than any World Series contest. I had less time for the Cubs or Colts. I noticed, too, that these clubs were not as benevolent as I had once believed. They were guilty of the same questionable hiring practices, the same avarice, as any other megamillion-dollar company doing big business in the United States.

The Colts, operated by a particularly greedy owner named Robert Irsay, deserted the loyal city of Baltimore in a most heartless manner in 1984. Irsay secretly loaded the Colts' equipment into a moving van and drove the franchise to

Indianapolis in the middle of one infamous March night. He kept the nickname and the horseshoe emblem, but these were not my Colts anymore. They played in a Midwest dome, a sterile palace that was not at all adorable. By now I was in mid-career as a journalist. I could not pretend to be stunned by these developments, and yet there was a twinge of sadness. Irsay had ransacked my old room, had torn down my wrinkled pennant.

The Cubs, meanwhile, were sold by the chewing-gum magnate Phil Wrigley to the cutthroat Tribune Company. Wrigley had never hired any African American managers or administrators. That had been bad enough. Now, the Tribune Company was demanding that lights be built at sacrosanct Wrigley Field, destroying decades of sunlit tradition so that night games could bring in bigger gates and profits. The Tribune threatened to move the team out of ivy-covered Wrigley Field if the city refused its ultimatum.

At the time, I was working at the *New York Daily News*, a Tribune Company-owned paper suffering through contraction pains and stripped naked of resources by its absentee managers. At the start of the recession, in October 1990, I went on a five-month strike forced upon the Newspaper Guild by an uncompromising, union-busting law firm hired by the Tribune. The enemy, very clearly to me, was the Tribune's board of directors; the very same board of directors that ruled over my favorite baseball team. While I walked the picket line at four o'clock in the morning, an existential question occurred to me: Were the dollars wrung from the Newspaper Guild being used to sign washed-up pitcher Danny Jackson to a free-agent contract?

I began to root against the Cubs. My reasoning held a desperate logic. I figured a poor performance by star second baseman Ryne Sandberg might adversely affect the Tribune stock price. That drop might force the company to negotiate with the union in good faith. Matters were

Illogical Loyalties

growing far too complicated. I grimaced whenever my son put on his Cubs' cap. I removed my autographed Ernie Banks baseball card from the refrigerator.

It soon dawned on me that such disloyalty represented a great, subversive danger to all of sports. Not just my singular action, of course. But the very notion that such alienation is possible ought to be very frightening to professional sports owners everywhere.

Fan loyalty is the engine that drives sports franchises. Without the long-term identification and devotion of the rabid customer, attendance and television ratings would decline steeply, fatally. The economy of pro leagues would sputter. If the Yankees or Celtics were viewed as simply another corporation that happened to make its headquarters temporarily in New York or Boston, fans would have little interest in following their activities over the long haul. They would feel free to switch brands according to quality, as they did with automobiles or breakfast cereals.

Who could blame them if they jumped ship? Fans certainly have every reason to turn away from the home team. The owners have rarely recognized their existence, except to mail them unilateral announcements about price hikes in ticket plans. Players view fans just as suspiciously, as fickle and sometimes crazy parasites who heap time demands upon them. When Bobby Bonilla of the Mets began wearing earplugs this season to blot out complaints from the home crowd at Shea, his act was one of tremendous symbolism.

Few fans realize in what low regard players and coaches hold them, and that is a good thing. I can remember, for example, Lee Elia's classic tirade against the Cub fans at Wrigley Field. Elia, the team's snakebitten manager, was annoyed at some impatient heckling from the Bleacher Bums. He launched a mean-tempered assault on the daylight faithful.

"Eighty-five percent of the people work, the other fifteen percent come out here [to watch Cub games]," Elia said, describing the Wrigley faithful in the crudest terms, something akin to "ignorant Yahoos." His coming out of the closet with his distaste for the paying customer undermined Elia's job security. He was soon fired. But subtler attacks occur after most games by players who are pestered for poor performances.

"Fans are going to think what they're going to think," Knick guard Gerald Wilkins once said. "They usually don't know what they're watching."

To the players, fans are autograph-demanding, tabloid-believing necessities of the trade. They help foot the bills. As Bill Laimbeer said, after the Piston center played the role of bad guy again at Boston Garden, "If I was them, I'd boo me, too. They pay for their tickets, they have a right to express themselves."

And they do pay. Ticket prices reach into triple-dollar figures for many showcase sporting events, and in the $50-$75 range for the best seats at relatively meaningless regular season games in pro basketball and hockey. The spectator explosion took root in the seventies, with network saturation on color television. It has not slowed, sprouting new outlets in every direction. Cable. Pay per view. Team-sponsored newsletter. The sports radio talk show, a phenomenon that did not catch on until about five years ago, is now a staple in most major American cities. Sports sections have expanded in newspapers as reluctant and staid as the *New York Times*.

The fans remain thirsty for statistics, for gossip, for expert analysis. Large-scale disaffection has occurred only rarely, when a franchise was about to flee a city. Then, and only then, the team is viewed as nothing more than a lame-duck widget factory. St. Louis gave the football Cardinals no support in their final season after the Cards had announced they were leaving for Phoenix. Eyes had been opened. This was no longer St. Louis's team. This was Bill Bidwell's franchise, no more or less than another McDonald's stand, and he was taking it elsewhere.

Illogical Loyalties

It takes a pie in the face sometimes before such realities are confronted. The lure of the ballpark can be blinding. Even the hard-edged businessman, after hours, can turn all gooey inside at the sight of a 400-foot homer. The fact is, however, that a sports franchise has little or nothing to do with the city or area in which it is housed. In many ways, the Japanese and Europeans are far more honest about this relationship. Japanese baseball teams are named after their parent corporations—the Yomiuri (newspaper company) Giants, not the Tokyo Giants. The same is true of Italian League basketball teams, such as Il Messaggero (another newspaper company) in Rome. Top soccer clubs throughout Germany, England, and Italy all wear advertisements of their chief sponsors on the front of their jerseys, instead of team logos.

Back in America, Raiders' owner Al Davis has courted a handful of cities as potential hosts for his football team, blackmailing these communities for the best possible lease arrangement. George Steinbrenner has done the same to New York City, threatening to move his Yankees to New Jersey unless the mayor promised him a new parking lot. Yet we are asked to believe that these teams belong to their host cities; that it is not the Busch Cardinals, but the St. Louis Cardinals; that it is not the Paramount Knicks, but the New York Knicks.

The American fan buys into this deception, happily. The media are in large part to blame. Television broadcasters can be excused their excess adoration, because they are generally employees of the team. Newspaper editors have no such excuse. When the Mets fell behind to the Red Sox, 3 games to 2, in the 1986 World Series, the *New York Daily News* ran a bold front-page headline, "WE AIN'T DEAD YET." A sound journalist might have assumed that the newspaper was referring to its own shaky financial situation. Instead, it was simply hyping the Mets, exhibiting total identification with a corporation that happened to manufacture baseball games in Flushing, Queens.

The editor of that paper might have argued, correctly, that he was merely giving his readers what they wanted. In my thirteen years of covering sports events for three different newspapers, I have witnessed a rabid, illogical loyalty to the home team. Behavior can border on the absurd, particularly among adults, and it manifests itself in ways that are peculiar to each sport:

American hockey fans seem more hostile to the opposition than they are supportive of their own team. Denis Potvin of the Islanders was serenaded for years with vicious chants by Ranger fans at Madison Square Garden. Fights break out in the stands as often as they do on the ice.

Pro basketball fans never stop berating the referees for foul calls against their team. Late in one game against the Knicks at Boston Garden in 1990, Boston fans loudly jeered a whistle against Larry Bird, even though Bird's foul had been intentional and helped to stop the clock.

Football fans, frigid and inebriated, like to cloak themselves in mascot items. Redskin fans, to support their "Hawgs," don pig masks. College football fans dress in garish colors and nutty disguises to match their college nicknames. Spectators sneak alcohol into stadiums, so they don't have to bother with the high-priced beer.

Baseball fans, with much time to kill between pitches and innings, entertain themselves with chants, songs, and the Wave. They are less likely to rebel over a bad call than over a long line at the hot-dog stand.

These fans are all very different, as are their passionate, dangerous European and South American soccer counterparts. But the strand of loyalty tethers all together. Rooting, as one, for the home team, must satisfy some basic human need to conform and act in concert. By cheering for the same team that we supported as children, we retain a nostalgic link to our past. Since the majority of fans are too old, or too young, to be in high school and college, we

Illogical Loyalties

require a local professional team to fulfill our membership needs.

Filmmaker Spike Lee went to the 1990 Super Bowl and came away from that experience with a darker analysis. He was truly frightened by the spectacle.

"It was like a big Nazi rally, all these people standing and waving flags together," he said.

By a fairly early age, and surely by high school, most of us come to an understanding with our own nature; we know whether we are cheerleader, or class rascal. Lee, I am quite sure, was never one to talk about school spirit or drum up support for the homecoming parade. And yet, even this practiced cynic sits front row to cheer the Knicks during most home games at Madison Square Garden.

If Lee can find some solace, some escape, some innocence in his neighborhood professional sports team, there might even be hope left for me. Maybe after I retire from this racket, the Cubbies will come to resemble teddy bears again. For now, they look like the Tribune Company, selling at 40 dollars per share on the New York Stock Exchange.

THE RITUAL LIFE OF SPORTS

JAMAKE HIGHWATER

Jamake Highwater has no record of where or when he was born. He was adopted at age seven and was raised and educated in southern California.

Mr. Highwater is a celebrated novelist, poet, essayist, and commentator on myth, music, dance, and the visual arts. He has been a member of the Executive Board of PEN, general director of the month-long Festival Mythos, and a guest lecturer at universities nationwide. He is the founder and president of the Native Land Foundation and the general director of the Native Arts Festival. Mr. Highwater has written more than twenty books. His work has appeared in the *New York Times*, *Esquire*, and the *Christian Science Monitor*, among others. His awards include an honorary doctorate from the Minneapolis College of Art and Design in 1986, the Best Film of the Year Award of the National Educational Film Festival in 1984, and in 1977 an American Library Association Newbury Honor Award. In 1979, Mr. Highwater was given the honorific name Piitai Sahkomaapii (Eagle Son) by an elder of the Blackfoot Indians in recognition of his scholarship in Native American subject matter.

Mr. Highwater divides his time between Hampton, Connecticut, and Los Angeles, California.

The Ritual Life of Sports

Baseball was originally played during the winter solstice, that critical time of the year for primal people when the days begin to lengthen and the dead earth starts to come back to life. According to anthropologist Leo Frobenius, the two teams of the ancient European ballgame were named Winter and Summer, and each team attempted to gain control of the ball, called "the sun." Thus, the ballgame that eventually became America's most characteristic sport has its roots in an early religious ceremony depicting what was, for primal people, the awesome battle between summer and winter, life and death, fertility and barrenness.

This ritualistic basis of sports is often ignored or neglected. "There seems to be a widespread failure (or refusal) to appreciate how much the element of ritual enters into our own publicly staged sports contests. In all human societies, rituals, festivals, dances, music, pictorial art, sports and games not only give pleasure but in addition provide outlets for creativity and reinforce the group identity and solidarity. Such activities also tie closely into social, religious, economic, and other phases of life. Whether at a given time in history [people] play for fun and self-expression, for prestige, power, and glory, for financial gain or political advantage, [their] motivations are to a large degree culturally determined," writes historian Florence Stumpf Frederickson.

But such culture determination differs from place to place and from time to time. For many years, our view of the world was sharply limited by the naive assumption that "human nature" is homogeneous. This attitude led us to surmise that all human thinking proceeds from a common set of premises and that all people are motivated by the same goals and needs. It was the repudiation of the notion of human nature being everywhere the same that led to the shattering of our inclination to judge the achievements and merits of the entire world by our own standards and expectations.

What we have learned is that our perception of things changes constantly because our vision of the world changes. We have come to recognize that our interpretation of the world is modeled upon archetypes called paradigms that give expression to our most fundamental view of ourselves and the cosmos. Societies are built upon these ever-changing paradigms. Every aspect of a culture is a reflection of the motivating and fundamental worldview that gives life to a civilization. Sports are one of the most vivid reflections of that persistent upheaval of our vision of ourselves and our world. We *are* the sports we play.

In ancient Greece, there was no effort to break records at the Olympic games because the Greeks kept no records. This lack of interest in record-keeping may seem peculiar to us today, obsessed as we are with computation and calibration. But for the Hellenic people there were only winners and losers. How one winner compared to previous winners did not concern them in the least. In fact, sports records were not kept until the Industrial Revolution in England, which was about the time the stopwatch was invented. But we must not assume that keeping records was simply the result of having an accurate device for measuring time. The larger picture is probably more to the point: The paradigm at the core of nineteenth-century England that brought about the Industrial Revolution and the invention of the stopwatch was also the motivating mentality that envisioned the unique idea of keeping records of sporting victories.

The role of sports in our own society is little understood. There has always been a deep love of recreation in America, but the attitude toward it has been curiously inhibited. During much of the history of the United States, recreation for its own sake was not entirely respectable. Emphasis was always placed on the idea that sports are work. As we know, the Puritans were bitterly hostile to sports. And Americans are notorious for their disdain for wasting time. Therefore many sports and diversions were rationalized as *useful* endeavors; for instance, proponents argued that sports enhance the health and strength of workers and therefore contribute to the productivity of the labor force. Among America's earliest sports were practical activities like barn-raisings and corn-husking contests. Because such sports were productive, they were not considered wasted efforts. Even the pleasures of hunting and fishing were justified as contributing to the food supply. Frederickson has pointed out that "rather overwhelming evidence exists of a profound cultural change with regard to sports and physical recreation in present-day American culture. Only a few localities remain in which it is not possible or entirely acceptable for adult men and women to go forth with golf clubs, tennis rackets, fishing reels, skis, or what-have-you for no other reason than the pursuit of pleasure. This trend in our culture seems to be the result of more than a lessening of puritanical objection to pleasure for pleasure's sake. Rather it is, according to many students of our society, a shift in fundamental objectives and goals. From an era when character was largely formed for work and at work, we have shifted to an era in which character is increasingly formed for leisure and during leisure." Today we are a nation that is much more fascinated by "idols of consumption" than by "idols of production."

What does all this mean? It suggests several things. For one, sports have been a human obsession for thousands of years. For another, the kind of games we play tells us a great deal about who we are, for, again, we *are* the games we play. And those games change as our world and our worldview change.

In the most critical sense, we do not exist in the same cosmos in which people existed before the time of Copernicus and Galileo, and we do not live in the same world that people lived in before Columbus and the age of exploration. The reality of our day is essentially different from what people meant by reality before Einstein, Freud, and Marx. Such revolutionary awakenings into new worlds of meaning are simply the most obvious and recent twists and turns of history. The essayist Ralph Waldo Emerson once said that "the whole of nature is a metaphor of the human mind." He could have been talking about the games we play, for they too are metaphors of the human mind at any given moment of history. We create sports and manipulate them to reflect the values of our ever-changing "model paradise."

Sports are visible clues to the paradigm of each era and each environment of human history. We are mirrored in the sports we play. They are microcosms that we create in our own image, expressing roles and ideals, providing rituals that seem to give us access to the unknowable and the indeterminate cosmos. We project models of our minds upon every aspect of our world. Ritual, religion, politics, and economics are infusions of our constantly changing visions of ourselves. We call one of these palpable visions "sport" as if it were an external reality, whereas it is simply a projection of who we think we are at a given moment in time. Sport, however, is not an illusion. It has substance in our thoughts. It is a lump of clay that we fashion into a replica of our own minds.

Originally, most games were used as ordeals of life and death, as forms of divination for making decisions that had immense social and emotional impact upon societies. Sport originated as an ambiguous expression of the most impulsive of human feelings and needs, which were later transformed into specific rituals with meticulous rules enforced by powerful religious referee-priests. As cultures changed and these rituals were transformed into the competitive social games we know today, the memory of their origins faded but their profound social power persisted. Despite our forgetfulness, sport continues into our century as a powerful and obsessive crowd activity. For instance, football apparently began as a territorial wargame and has been gradually transformed over the centuries into one of the most popular of modern contact sports. Once football had an important religious function as a form of divination—a competitive ordeal between two teams (or towns or tribes) to determine matters of life and death. These ancient functions of the game from which football arose have been subtly replaced by other social functions of which we are hardly aware: an expression of the crowd as a political, economic, and predominantly male force in our new middle-class society.

The games various societies play tell us a great deal about their core mentality and motivation—their "worldview." Sport makes prehistory and mythology visible to us and demonstrates how traces of ancient belief and ritual have survived in the games we play.

We cannot fail to recognize among the sports of humankind a revelation that is probably one of the greatest realizations of the twentieth century: that mythologies and the activities reflecting them are the anvil upon which human mentality distinguished itself, upon which it names itself, and ultimately knows itself.

The poet Ezra Pound, in 1937, wrote that "it has taken us two thousand years to get round again to meditating on mythology." Almost fifty years later, this remark is still powerfully suggestive. As historian Herbert L. Schneidau has said, "It may be that the most important development of twentieth-century consciousness has to do not with atom bombs or moon walks, but with a new seriousness toward prehistory and mythology." We are rediscovering the capacity to recognize realities that exist outside our own empiricist frame of mind, and we have developed a mentality that permits us to grasp the meaning of hitherto neglected games and rites of prehistory and of primal societies. Sport is the legacy of this intricate interface between mythology and ritual, and simultaneously a window that allows us to look back at our past.

The imagination illuminates and, finally, defines our *only* reality—the only truth we can know. That light is a mythic lantern. And the world that it illuminates for us is the realm of ritual by which we know ourselves, what we have been, and what we are becoming.

Sports evolved out of the universal impulse to play.

Many cultural historians believe that play is the basis of ritual and religion as well as theater, music, poetry, and dance. In the company of such civilized achievements, athletic activity assumes a cultural role of considerable importance, "as a repository for idealized values of the society," writes historian Jan Felshin.

The remarkable theatrical innovator Antonin Artaud thought of the actor as "an athlete of the emotions." Many sociologists compare games to ritual reenactments of combat. Psychologists have often noted the inclination of all animals—especially the young—to release exuberant energy in playful activities. Some even see play as a sort of divine madness.

The connection between sport and play is very interesting, but it is also something of a puzzlement because of the ambiguous nature of play. Even the derivation of the word *play* is perplexing. It comes from the Anglo-Saxon *plega*, which has a wide variety of meanings. In its oldest form, it signified "to take risks, to expose oneself to danger for something or someone." The words *pledge* and *plight* are in the same etymological family. Such associations are both unexpected and fascinating in relation to the way we usually think of play.

The Ritual Life of Sports

The abundance of different meanings of the word *play* is a source of considerable difficulty for those of us trying to understand how and why play relates to sports, religious ritual, theater, dance, music, and poetry. We speak of waves *playing* on the beach and of children *playing* baseball. Actors *play* parts in *plays*. Musicians *play* music by *playing* their instruments. People *play* chess, checkers, and cards (but, curiously, they shoot dice). At the racetrack people *play* the horses. In Homer the gods *play* with mortals, while mortals *play* cat and mouse with one another. Opossums *play* dead. Erotic people *play* with themselves. And lovers *play* with one another by engaging in *foreplay*.

Such a lively variety of usages of a single word prompts many to dismiss the possibility that there is any fundamental and meaningful connection between all forms of "play." And, if such a connection does not exist, what can we make of the observation that sports seem to be born of the impulse to play?

As historian Marie Hart has observed, "the slippery task of defining and differentiating among the concepts of play, game, and sport has tantalized many writers." The renowned Dutch medievalist Johan Huizinga was one of the first scholars to investigate the theme of "Man the Player." In his *Homo Ludens*, Huizinga argues that play is the fundamental source of human cultural behavior. "The spirit of playful competition is, as a social impulse, older than culture itself and pervades all life like a veritable ferment," he wrote in 1938. "Ritual grew up in sacred play; poetry was born in play and nourished on play; music and dancing were pure play. Wisdom and philosophy found expression in words and forms derived from religious contests. The rules of warfare, the conventions of noble living were built up in play patterns. We have to conclude, therefore, that civilization is, in its earliest phases, played. It does not come from play like a babe detaching itself from the womb; it arises in and as play, and never leaves it."

Huizinga's comments go a long way to illuminate the potential impact of play on society, but he says very little about play in relation to sport. In fact, he did not greatly concern himself with sport; and he made no attempt to make a connection between play and sport. He did, however, maintain that play is a central element in athletics. One of his most significant ideas is the belief that cultures become empty and passionless when activities such as sport, philosophy, poetry, and the performing arts lose their sense of playfulness. Here, I think we can understand that by "playfulness" Huizinga means something very close to philosopher F. S. C. Northrop's concept of "aesthetic immediacy."

In *The Meeting of East and West*, Northrop writes, "To an Oriental, a Western painter always seems to have painted the object from the outside, whereas the Oriental paints it with feeling and with identification of the artist with it from within." In the same fashion, playfulness momentarily raises us above the world of the complacent and theoretical. Playfulness becomes a state of mind that frees us from the theoretical, external world and allows us to know the world from within—not as an object of thought, but as an instantaneous and immediate experience.

Religious mysticism, art, and play are often regarded as activities that transcend the natural world. "Like art and religion, play is not far from the feast...for play celebrates the emergence of a finite world that lies outside and beyond the world of nature while at the same time resting upon it," Kenneth L. Schmitz has written in his fine essay "Sport and Play: Suspension of the Ordinary."

Such remarks open the way to a significant relationship between the illusive world of play and the ritualized world of sport. As historian Paul Weiss has noted, "The athlete comes to accept his body as himself. This requires him to give up, for the time being, any attempt to allow his mind to dwell on objectives that are not germane to what his body is, what it needs, and what it can or ought to do."

We can say exactly the same thing of the painter who accepts his painting as himself, for he must become the painting in order to paint it. So too the dancer becomes the dance. The writer, the composer, and the mystic experience this same transformational process.

As rarefied as it may seem to speak of an athlete in such abstract terms, in fact such transformation is not rare. Every child has an intense and intimate knowledge of it. Play builds illusion. Huizinga calls our attention to the fact that the Latin word for play, *ludus*, is very much like *inlusio*, illusion. "The 'inactuality' of play is most evident in the imaginative play of make-believe," writes Schmitz. "This suspension of the 'real' world by means of a play-decision releases a world of 'unreality' which needs no justification from outside itself. It is a self-sealed world, delivering its own values in and for itself." As a work of art requires no defense or explanation but itself, so too play is justified unto itself. "Play cannot vindicate itself except to one who plays. To anyone else it appears superfluous. The stern Calvin Coolidge, it is said, once snorted that going fishing is childish, which only proved to fishermen that he was absurd." Play is a world unto itself, with its own built-in rationale. In this way it may be said that play is objectless insofar as it has no other object than itself.

Like mysticism and art, play embodies a significance that is not linear and logical. It does not lend itself to analysis any more than does a work of art. As an analysis does not explain or replace a painting or a dance, so a description of its rules or its make-believe is not a substitute for play. But analysis may clarify the genuine internalized, self-contained, and nonlinear reality of play. As Schmitz points out, *the proper vehicle of meaning in play is action*, and in this way play and its various manifestations as sport are much closer to ritual and myth than to technology and linear mentality. Play, like dance and ritual, "is meaning embodied in action." It is "significant form" (Huizinga) because it perfectly reflects the shape of the impulses that govern bodily movement and feeling. Writes Schmitz, "The world which opens out through the play-decision is a world of possibilities closed off from the natural and ordinary world. Measured against the ordinary world, the world of possibility opened up by play seems inactual and illusory; but measured in terms of being itself, it is a radical way of being human, a distinctive mode of being. It is a way of taking up the world of being, a manner of being present in the world in the mode of creative possibility whose existential presence is a careless joyful freedom."

But let us not allow ourselves to be overtaken by a rampantly romantic notion of play. Seriousness is not the opposite of play. Games are usually taken very seriously by everyone who plays them, because the special reality created in the context of a game is somehow very important to us. And thus, Huizinga points out, the cheat is far less chastised than the spoilsport, who totally subverts and shatters the make-believe reality of the game. Nor is play solely the entertainment of a garden of delights. For play also has its "agonistic elements," which can be seen in many cultures that openly depend upon organized competitions and contests as social processes. Such "war-play"—even if its outcome is highly destructive—has been a strong motivating force throughout world history. One thinks of the "Flowery Wars" of the Aztecs during which friendly enemies regularly staged prearranged raids upon one another for the purpose of obtaining sacrificial victims; the *potlatch* of the Pacific Northwest Coast tribes during which massive amounts of valued goods were publicly destroyed in a flamboyant effort to demonstrate wealth and rank; feudal combat and stylized blood baths such as the Battle of Fontenoy of the *ancien régime;* or a medieval tourney or a samurai duel.

Florence Frederickson has demonstrated that wrestling, one of the most ancient of sports, has had many different historical roles: as a legal and judicial mechanism for settling the boundaries of rice fields in the Philippines and villages in Pukapuka, as part of initiation and puberty rites, as a means of selecting a mate, as a demonstration of the power of a tribal leader, and as a means of securing an abundant harvest. For instance, trial by wrestling was a custom throughout Ifugao, particularly to settle disputes over rice-field boundaries. The rationale behind the wrestling trials was that the ancestral spirits knew which party was in the right and where the true boundary lay and would therefore see to it that the person in the right would win. In Pukapuka, the rights of puberty ended with a wrestling match, after which the boys were considered to be men. Among the Dukawa of Nigeria it was the custom for women to select their husbands at wrestling matches. Ancient Hawaiian chiefs kept a stable of wrestlers as a valued part of their retinue. When a visiting chief was expected, it was the custom to welcome him by arranging a match at which host and guest were each represented by his finest wrestler.

Marshall McLuhan, in *Understanding Media*, reminds us that "games are dramatic models of our psychological lives providing releases of our particular tensions." He recalls a 1963 article about Papua New Guinea in *Life* magazine: "The traditional enemies of the Willigiman-Wallalua are the Wittaia, a people exactly like themselves in language, dress, and custom...Every week or two the Willigiman-Wallalua and their enemies arrange a formal battle at one of the traditional fighting grounds. In comparison with the catastrophic conflicts of 'civilized' nations, these frays seem more like a dangerous field sport than true war. Each battle lasts but a single day, always stops before nightfall (because of the danger of ghosts) or if it begins to rain (no one wants to get his hair or ornaments wet). The men are very accurate with their weapons...but they are equally adept at dodging, hence are rarely hit by anything...This perpetual bloodshed is carried on for none of the usual reasons for waging war. No territory is won or lost; no goods or prisoners seized. They fight because they enthusiastically enjoy it...and because they feel they must satisfy the ghosts of slain companions."

The codes of behavior of mutual massacre strongly resemble those of play. The historian Peter C. McIntosh reminds us that as late as 1829 a Frenchman passing through Derby and witnessing a game of English football remarked: "If Englishmen call this playing, it would be difficult to imagine what they would call fighting!"

In short, play can be brutal. But, as we have come to realize at the end of "war-play" and the beginning of the first total war (by which I mean the American Civil War, when for the first time and on a large scale cities became battlefields and civilians became targets), war is far more brutal when it loses its ritualized and restraining "rules of the game" and gives itself over to unbridled destruction and aggression. There may be something fundamentally stupid and repulsive about the antiquated notion of the "gentleman soldier," but such ritualized deportment even in war provided the West with a basis of restraint. Even terrible waste of life and property, when governed by social ritual with mutually agreed and binding rules, can be essential to a cultural process—military, artistic, political, economic. Many historians have noted that society seems to advance through struggle, as long as there are rules of the game that keep aggression within the bounds of survival. Today perhaps the most fearsome aspect of our international situation, when we most need some limits in the use of the truly terrible arsenal of weapons we possess, is the realization that our leaders no longer believe in the rules of war.

The agonistic element of play should not be understood as a justification of violence. But neither can we neglect the aggressive nature of play; otherwise we will never be able to comprehend the highly competitive and often brutal aspects of sport (or, for that matter, the performing and visual arts) in the twentieth century. An inescapable element of tension may be central to all forms of play. In games we frequently set up some kind of tension as a form of challenge. There is no society that does not have diversions in which participants arrange purely artificial obstacles and get satisfaction and social recognition by overcoming them. And we need not explore history to any great extent before recognizing that most societies are governed by "rules of play." In fact, as Huizinga points out, such civilizations are "play-communities." Perhaps this relationship between play and culture exists because the mentality of games provides a necessary ritual that embodies the transformation of tension (chaos and uncertainty) into order.

"Play creates order; play is order," Huizinga tells us. "Into an imperfect world and into the confusion of life it brings a temporary, a limited perfection. Play demands order absolute and supreme. The least deviation from it 'spoils the game.'"

The order that is implicit in play results in an implicit tension, caused by concern that the rules of the game might be broken. As the French philosopher Paul Valery observed: "No skepticism is possible where the rules of a game are concerned, for the principle underlying them is an unshakeable truth." In fact, if the rules are broken, then the whole play-world collapses, and the game is over.

Without such make-believe rules there can be no play. And there can be no society. Play has its own time and space, boundaries and objectives, rewards and penalties.

Jamake Highwater

The conventions and rules of a sport suspend the ordinary rules of life, and for the duration of the game the new law is the only one that counts, according to McIntosh. It is a distinctive way, voluntary and finite, of being-in-the-world. Playing in the world, we recover ourselves as "free and transcendent beings," in Schmitz's words.

Some of us may have problems with aspects of Johan Huizinga's brilliant essays on play, but there is no question that his concepts provide a core of motivation and meaning for the variety and diversity of games, sports, and diversions. Huizinga also suggests the subtle psychological process that transforms child's play into adult ritual. Children's games, he points out, may seem to be mere shams, but in fact they are actualizations of appearances, full of imagination. "The child is *making an image* of something different, something more beautiful, or more sublime, or more dangerous than what he usually is. His representation is not so much a sham-reality as a *realization in appearance*. Passing now from the children's games to the sacred performances in archaic culture, we find that there is more of a mental element 'at play.' The sacred performance is more than a sham-reality or an actualization in appearance. It is also more than a symbolical actualization. It is a mystical expression. In it something invisible and inactual takes beautiful, actual, holy form."

At their great seasonal rites, all the world's people observe the cyclical drama of the natural world: the change of seasons, the phases of the moon, night turning into day with the rebirth of the sun, the motions of the constellations, the germination and ripening of the crops, as well as birth, life, and death of beasts and people. As Frobenius puts it, primal societies *play* the order of nature as imprinted in their consciousness. Rituals are sacred games in and through which we actualize, or recreate, the events of nature and thus help to maintain the order of the cosmos.

Essential to this ritualization of the imprint of nature

The Ritual Life of Sports

upon our consciousness is the creation of a closed space, marked off either actually or ideally so that it is outside reality. Inside this space the ritual is played. Inside this space the rules of the game are supreme. Yet this hallowed place is actually a "playground." For, "formally speaking, there is no distinction whatever between marking out a space for a sacred purpose and marking it out for purposes of sheer play. The turf, the tennis court, the chessboard, and pavement-hopscotch cannot formally be distinguished from the temple or the magic circle," says Huizinga.

From play comes ritual. And from ritual comes sport.

Psychologically, we know that sports arise, at least in part, from the play impulse. Historically, however, we are not certain exactly how, where, and when specific athletic activities came into existence. We can only imagine the chronology and process by which the complex contests, games, and rules that we now associate with athletic activities first came into being.

Many scholars firmly believe that the world of prehistory was a world of hunters, warriors, and priests and that out of the aggression and skills associated with hunting and warring there evolved elaborate religious rites that became symbols of the grand metaphysical battles tribal peoples fight against the unknown. Physicist Paul Davies tells us that in the past human beings viewed the world as a "temperamental place, full of caprice and random occurrences." A dangerous and unpredictable place. A place that offered no assurances that the great glowing sun that had died at dusk would be reborn at dawn, or that the fruitful plants that perished in autumn would be miraculously reborn in the spring. Theirs was a world filled with dreadful and delightful puzzlements, many of which continue to perplex us: conception, birth, death, dreams, feelings, mind. These shadows of the unknown are the enemies that primal people battle in their metaphysical wars called rituals.

"Virtually every competitive sport in the modern world is a refinement of physical contests originating in ancient and medieval times. Taking their form largely from hunting and warring activities necessary for survival, competitive games began primarily as religious rituals designed to win the favor of the gods or to honor the memories of heroic leaders. Over the centuries the sacred aspect diminished. But whether in front of tribal totems, at the Egyptian temples of Osiris, beside Greek altars to Zeus, before the Roman pantheon, under the Mohammedan banner of Allah, or in the medieval Christian monasteries and church cloisters, sports evolved always in relation to religious ceremonies, holidays, and institutions," writes historian William F. Baker.

A curious collection of smooth, lemon-shaped stones may provide us with one of our few glimpses of the prehistoric moment when sports evolved out of the skills and aggressive behavior of hunters and warriors. Paleoanthropologists are familiar with fossil bones having microscopic scratch marks, suggesting that at least two million years ago human beings were eating meat butchered from animal carcasses. But experts do not understand the significance of the smooth, roundish stones that also litter human sites such as Olduvai Gorge in Tanzania.

"It has become increasingly apparent that the flaked stone tools of that era were used for cutting, not fighting," Barbara Isaac of the Peabody Museum at Harvard told *Discovery* magazine. "So how did our ancestors hunt these animals? Or, if they were scavengers, how did they keep other scavengers away?"

The answer, Isaac and other experts have suggested, may be those lemon-shaped stones lying at scientists' feet.

Guessing that the stones could have been weapons, Isaac began a search of early chronicles of encounters with tribal peoples. Just as she suspected, she found a report by the

French explorer of the South Pacific, Count de la Perouse, in which he recounts the loss of twelve of his sixty-one men during a 1787 voyage to Samoa (then called the Navigators Islands). The men, who had gone ashore for water, were suddenly caught in a fusillade of rocks thrown, according to the count, "so hard they produced almost the same effect as our bullets, and had the advantage of succeeding one another with great rapidity."

Later, in 1870, J. G. Wood wrote in *The Natural History of Man* that aborigines in Australia had occasionally killed British soldiers by unleashing "a shower of stones...with such force and precision that must be seen to be believed."

Intrigued by Wood's report, Isaac eventually located nine Pacific Island "war handstones" in the collection of the Pitt River Museum at Oxford. Such handstones were also found at the Museum of Mankind in London and at the Peabody. Most of these projectiles were shaped like lemons, suggesting that they were thrown with a spin, "rather like tiny footballs."

The hands of early human beings were well suited to throwing stones. According to physical anthropologist Mary Marzke, "our ancestors as far back as the 3.5 million-year-old Lucy could shape their hands into the three-fingered grip that baseball pitchers use for strength and control." A familiar technique used to produce a fast ball!

Throwing stones seems to come so naturally to *homo sapiens* that "it could have been a principle incentive for our forebears to walk upright," say biological anthropologists Eileen O'Brien and Charles Peters of the University of Georgia. And the impulse to throw things, adds Isaac, is still very much alive today. "Modern ball sports seem perfect for channeling this aggressive behavior."

The Marxist sport historian Gerhard Lukas has suggested that the first sport was not rock-throwing but spear-throwing. According to Lukas, "sport is not play...It is only a preparation for work and a reflection of the needs of a creative animal to survive and progress." The argument is impressive but ultimately suffers from the outdated notion that *homo sapiens* are the only tool-using animals—a stance overthrown by primate behavioral research. Lukas's Marxist perception of sport is echoed by the German Marxist Bero Rigauer, who sees modern athletics not as work, but as "demoralized work," involving discipline, authority, competition, accomplishment, and bureaucracy. In short, sports for Rigauer are a reflection of industrial capitalism.

This political view of sports may have validity in the essential aspects of sports as we know them in our own era, for modern sports "first appeared in England when that society, and not merely coincidentally, was beginning to undergo the Industrial Revolution. Modern sports, therefore, are particular adaptations to modern economic, social, and political life," writes historian Richard D. Mandell.

As contested as it may be, the Marxist idea of Gerhard Lukas—that sport was a primordial invention as a preparation for work—is a good deal more acceptable than the widely held romantic notion of classical revisionists "that sport appeared gloriously and spontaneously during the golden age of Greece and then suddenly and tragically disappeared, waiting to be brought to life again in our own times," in Mandell's words.

Carl Diem's world history of sports, *Weltgeschichte des Sports* opens with the statement: "All physical exercises were originally cultic." And, indeed, there is an abundance of evidence to support the claim that primal societies often incorporated jumping, running, wrestling, throwing, and even playing ball in their rituals and ceremonies. As the historian Allen Guttman points out, so pervasive is athletic activity in the complex of theater-dance-ritual in tribal societies that most such groups do not have a word for sport. There is also ample evidence that sports and games metaphorically reflect the material culture of a

The Ritual Life of Sports

society. Hunting-gathering people tend to transform stalking and killing skills into athletic activities: both to celebrate the achievements and prowess of the hunter and to prepare the young for adult roles as hunters. Agricultural peoples, who usually transpose their metaphysical focus from the giving earth to the signs of the heavens, devote much of their athletic activity to celestial games, or "games of the sky."

Writing about the Timbira Indians of Brazil, for instance, historian Kathe Hye-Kerdal emphasizes the connection between sport and the worldview of a people. One Timbira sport, a relay race, is performed by two teams. One represents the sun; the other, the moon. The track on which the race is run is called "the Milky Way" after the heavenly course over which the sun and the moon had carried out their original mythic competition. The ceremony itself is clearly more important to the participants than winning or losing.

There are games of the earth, matriarchal in focus and devoted to the mother goddesses of life and death, and games of the sky, patriarchal in focus and devoted to the gods of law and reason. There are also war games, like those already described between the Willigiman-Wallalua and the Wittaia of Papua New Guinea; these are often devoted to a contest between earth and sky.

A drastic shift from the earth orientation associated with the mother goddess, who was dominant from approximately 25,000 BC, to the sky orientation took place in approximately 2500 BC throughout the Near East and the Balkans with the emergence of a patriarchal sun/sky deity variously called Adonis and Apollo. Although it is difficult to be specific about the cause of it, the subsequent shift from games of the earth to games of the sky would seem to be evidence of a waning of conscious ritualism within a society, a shift from faith and intuition to logic and reason, a shift from ritual play to sport.

Jamake Highwater

This transition from play to sport is less apparent than the transformation of religious rituals into secularized sports. But as Guttman indicates, the much later secularization of rituals is a transition that we can grasp in terms of our own experience of relatively recent history. "When one speaks of secularization, one does not mean that an originally religious phenomenon becomes worldly but rather that an athletic game originally laden with religious significance concentrated itself upon its own essential elements—play, exercise, competition. Sports gradually become a part of the ordinary life of the *polis* as well as a means of worship...Whether or not one considers the passions, the rituals, and the myths of modern sport as a secular religion, the fundamental contrast with [primal] and ancient sports remains. The bond between the secular and the sacred has been broken, the attachment to the realm of the transcendent has been severed. We do not run in order that the earth be more fertile. We till the earth, or work in our factories and offices, so that we can have time to play."

Johan Huizinga is the preeminent source of this somewhat gloomy assessment of the late twentieth century that scholars like Guttman have explored and amplified. As such, Huizinga has been much maligned as an elitist because in the 1930s, when he wrote his classic work on the element of play in culture, *Homo Ludens*, he was capable of foreseeing the terrible consequences of the loss of playfulness as a driving force in society. He detested the secularization of society: the concretizing of our mythologies, the reckless abandonment of our visionary mentalities, the victory of mediocrity in art, religion, and political life. For him the world went sour in the nineteenth century: "All Europe donned the boiler-suit. Henceforth the dominants of civilization were to be social consciousness, educational aspirations, and scientific judgment...This grotesque overestimation of the economic factor was conditioned by our worship of technological progress, which was itself the fruit of rationalism and utilitarianism after they had killed the mysteries and acquitted man of guilt and sin." But, Huizinga insists, such acquittal is purely illusory, for the scientific materialism that destroyed orthodox religious faith is so complex that those foolish enough to believe in Original Sin can never completely believe in their acquittal. As a consequence, they are stripped of the visionary gift their mythology provided at the same time that they continue to be burdened by a fanatic sense of religious guilt.

For Huizinga, the modern world is a wasteland. Stripped of sacredness and playfulness, humankind is left with nothing but the terror of its dehumanized and playless world of industry and petty commerce.

As historian George Steiner comments in his introduction in the 1970 edition of *Homo Ludens*, "The uncomfortable truth may be that high culture, with its achievements in the arts, literature, and pure thought, does depend on such hierarchic, ritualized models of society as Periclean Athens, Tudor England, or the France of Louis XIV. Conceivably, social progress and a more equitable distribution of economic resources militate against aesthetic and speculative virtuosity. Huizinga may be proved accurate in his prognostication that the culture of a consumer-democracy will differ sharply from that to which we owe our principle artistic and philosophical legacies."

In Western civilization, the power of art and religious ritual has been gradually displaced and abandoned as people have discovered cause and effect and pursued the control of nature by technological methods that alter the circumstances of their fundamental existence. At such a time, the power of religious rites and images ceases to be a prime object of the society. Sport persists, but it expresses itself on the basis of other aims and principles. As Guttman has observed: "Sports [can] take on a religious significance of their own. One of the strangest turns in the long, devious route that leads from...ritual to the World Series is the proclivity of modern sport to become a kind of secular faith."

Ironically, the process of civilization as we know it may be contradictory to the process of art and ritual.

Running Backs and Running Dogs

John Krich

John Krich was born in New York City in 1951. He headed west to attend Reed College in Portland, Oregon, but at the age of nineteen decided to drop out. A year later, he had finished his first novel and moved to San Francisco.

Mr. Krich is a novelist, journalist, travel writer, sports writer, and California historian. He is the author of six books. His novel *A Totally Free Man* won a special citation of the PEN/Hemingway Award in 1981 for best first novel. His books *Music in Every Room: Around the World in a Bad Mood*, and *El Beisbol* were finalists for the Quality Paperback Book Club New Literary Voices Award and the Casey Award, respectively. Mr. Krich was awarded literary fellowships by the National Endowment for the Arts in 1979 and 1992. His writing has appeared in *Mother Jones*, the *New York Times*, and *Sports Illustrated*, among other publications.

Mr. Krich lives in the San Francisco Bay area. He is currently working on a novel about mail-order brides.

Running Backs and Running Dogs

"*We must learn to look at problems all-sidedly, seeing the reverse as well as the obverse in things. In given conditions, a bad thing can lead to good results and a good thing to bad results.*"
—Coach Mao Zedong, The Little Red Rule Book

Tiananmen Square is a perfect gridiron. Properly rectangular, level as the best-laid patch of Astroturf, this ultimate expression of the Chinese love for symmetry would be the dream site for America's most symmetrical sport. Creating a yin-yang bisection of territorial turf is Chang An, the Avenue of Eternal Peace, fifty-yard-line of the world's most populous playing field. The central Monument of the Martyrs of the Revolution is a veritable kicking tee for Chinese history. Lampposts outfitted with surveillance cameras serve as hash marks to pace off the vast distance of this stone playground, which, to use the All-American yardstick, is "as long as four football fields." There are even loudspeakers placed all around for announcing downs. Plenty of uniformed refs, too, for enforcing penalties. At either end, the matching red arches and immense tile overhangs of Beijing's ancient gates make perfect goal posts—protecting the Forbidden City. What an apt name for an end zone!

No wonder the first pigskin squads ever to set foot in the People's Republic cannot resist heading straight to Tiananmen for a mock scrimmage. Afterward, the coaches will claim that their choice was merely coincidental—that they had no idea their four-star hotel was so close to China's prime site for confrontations nearly as violent as the pastime they sought to import. Baggage unpacked, changed into matching sweats and gleaming Nikes, everyone bounds off for an unscheduled foray into Beijing. Whether naive or mischievous, these college kids and their whistle-toting mentors look for the nearest large space in which to air out passes and run deep fly patterns. The quarterbacks loosen the kinks in their jet-cramped arms. The wide receivers sprint down infinite sidelines. A fascinated crowd of gawkers gathers. (In China, they gather faster than anywhere on earth.) This is the last thing that the nervous authorities want on the week of the second anniversary of the massacre in the Square. While burly linemen do light hitting drills on the steps of Chairman Mao's Mausoleum, the soldiers begin shooing away the curious citizenry. The plainclothesmen swarm in, barking on their walkie-talkies. Heads are already beginning to roll in the Foreign Ministry. But this isn't a protest, the players will insist. They are just doing what comes naturally, serving up a sample of American spontaneity that their hosts don't know how to handle. As the expression goes, nobody wants this trip to be turned into a "political football." They don't know that, in Tiananmen Square, somebody is always keeping score.

"'Lifting a rock only to drop it on one's own feet' is a Chinese folk saying to describe the behavior of certain fools. The reactionaries in all countries are fools of this kind."
—Little Red Rule Book

It all sounded so good in the press release. After much negotiation and revisions in schedule, two perennial champions of the NAIA, or small-college second division, Pacific Lutheran University of Tacoma, Washington, and Evangel College of Springfield, Missouri, would have the honor of playing the first exhibition games of American football in the People's Republic of China. The Chinese call the sport "Oliveball," after the shape of the pigskin projectile, but they have hardly been exposed to the real

Running Backs and Running Dogs

thing outside a couple of telecasts of the Super Bowl and one teaching clinic offered by a few professional players. For twenty days, the Lutes and the Crusaders—perhaps for this occasion the fearless elevens should change their nicknames to the Marco Polos and the Kissingers—will hoist their shoulder pads around the far side of the world. Games are to be played in Beijing, Shanghai, and Canton, China's three largest cities, with "a sell-out crowd of 200,000" promised for the baptismal event in the capital's Workers' Stadium. Premier Li Peng and other high Chinese officials promise to be in attendance. At the announcement of the tour, Beijing's *People's Daily* touted this first opportunity for the masses to "watch great American football performance." And CCTV, China's national, state-run channel, plans to broadcast this beginning lesson in Xs and Os to a possible audience of half a billion potential Joe Montanas. How about Joe Guangzhou?

We do not think of the Chinese as great sportsmen. Their ancient culture produced no Olympian tradition and their participation in the modern version had, until recently, contributed but a few androgyne diving champions to international jock legend. Ping Pong and mah-jongg are hardly the domain of triathletes. Even Chinese checkers isn't really Chinese. "Friendship first, competition second!" was the cry advanced during the Cultural Revolution. But at the recent Asian Games, a public relations debacle that failed to promote Beijing's bid to host the Olympics, I sat among jingoist fans waving red banners and crowing over their first chance to defeat and outright bully the teams of their poorly trained and less populous neighbors. The host country made sure they swept every event, including such alien pursuits as baseball, badminton, and an ancient Indian form of tag called *kabbadi*. Credited with the invention of practically everything else on the planet, the Chinese can claim as their own no major team sport. But it's a different story when you talk about taking aim or taking sides, betting and strategizing and plotting next moves. Then the Chinese offer the best proof that sports is not the same as game-playing.

Writing their stirring announcements, the Athletic Directors of the two tiny American institutions did not consider that their hosts had not only invented paper but also the first deceptions of print. Who could blame these schools for jumping at the bait of staging the most significant cultural interchange and goodwill gesture in recent Sino-American history? This outing promised to be more than mere Ping Pong diplomacy. This would be a pigskin blitz—tackling and flattening the defensive demons of suspicion and misunderstanding. Never mind that hardly a tour group had dared make this trip since the crackdown that had occurred exactly two years earlier. Like missionaries of old, the finest young men of Evangel and Pacific Lutheran would further penetrate the breach in godless China with their clean-cut manners, quiet faith, and a few All-American knees-to-the-groin. As the road to hell is paved with good intentions, so, too, is the road to China.

"If you want knowledge, you must take part in the practice of changing reality. It you want to know the taste of a pear, you must change the pear by eating it yourself."

I can hardly fault the two teams, for I barely know what I am doing in China myself. If anything, my own mission is more illusory. In the beginning, it must have had something to do with deciphering the mysteries of the world's oldest and most gutted civilization. In youthful days, I viewed China as a model of proletarian purity and pig-tailed innocence, the one place on earth where deed matched word, especially when those words were Chairman Mao's campy homilies. But I have come to spend the summer in a China mired in lies, a land of closet capitalists still forced to wear socialist masks. With motives more obvious than any I've seen in the United States, this a culture unconflictedly committed to unblandished materialism. And finding the Chinese all too scrutable only throws me back into examining the more intractable mysteries lodged in my own psyche.

Besides, there isn't much else to do in Beijing, a city of ten million that provides but four movie theaters showing exciting shorts on the production of industrial cement, a smattering of coffee shoppes, a series of dueling all-you-can-eat buffets, and a couple of black-market watering holes to simulate the alien concept of nightlife. So I find myself bowling at four in the morning at the spiffy basement lanes of luxury hotel complexes. I take an excursion out to the newly dedicated Shenzhou Doggy Park, an only-in-China amusement center that exhibits common household poodles and schnauzers like rare species. In a land where man's best friend has long been man's best appetizer, this hands-on zoo offers kids the thrill of walking the mutt of their choice. Instead of doing the usual tricks, trained hounds are shown chasing down counter-revolutionaries. In one underlit indoor cave, a canine Emperor and Empress sit chained to uncomfortable thrones. There is no boxer rebellion.

Foreigners in China are still kept caged in high-rise kennels like some "imperialist running dogs," the ultimate Maoist insult. So, like the rest of my kind, I turn to running with the Hash House Harriers, an informal fraternity of expatriates who jog weekly at as many strange venues as can be found on the planet. One week, our T-shirted pack puffs its way between roller coaster rides at the Beijing Amusement Park—where the usual mistranslated signs warn, "Heart sufferers—please do not be amused!" After the hearty Harriers circle the smelly moat of the Imperial Palace, somebody gets the bright idea to set a course through the city's garbage dump. If a runner gives up, he or she has to chug Beijing beer from an antique Chinese hospital bedpan! We even stage a scavenger hunt along Wangfujing, the city's main shopping street, weaving out of stores and through bustling food stands in search of used chopsticks, baby socks, sour plum candies, or portraits of Chou En-lai. Perennially exhausted from their menial labors and endless bicycling, the locals gape at us like we're daft. And we revel in being those mad dogs and Englishmen who dare to run in the noonday sun. Living amidst the uniformity of brick compounds and cotton-suited communalism makes us Westerners want to flaunt our individualism, our allegiance to the irrational, and, above all, to that daring new religion that goes by the name of "leisure." Now this is a true cultural exchange: The more we shock the Chinese, the more we wake ourselves. When I hear about the upcoming football match, I can only hope to be further awakened.

"An army without culture is a dull-witted army, and a dull-witted army cannot defeat the enemy."

There is nothing stranger than crossing the mobile Chinese welter of a morning bicycle rush hour and stepping inside a hotel lobby crowded with corn-fed kids stalking about in cleats and shoulder pads. I catch up with the two teams just in time to head off with them for their one and only practice. Falling into a front seat of their bus, it strikes me that the Pacific Lutheran Lutes are a rather average lot of goofy, spunky Americans—open and unguarded, full of ass-pinching pranks and wise-ass remarks and an irrepressible irreverence toward all authority figures. Nearly to a man-boy, they are biting their lips at the excitement of being in China. And nothing thrills them more than finding out from Miss Wong, the bus translator, the Mandarin words for "Let's go!" Before long, the team travels everywhere to the incessant chant of "Zo ba! Zo ba!"

Few of the players have ever been anywhere outside their hometowns and college dorms in Tacoma—though it turns out this school prides itself on being ambassadors for football, having also played exhibitions in Italy some years back. "This is a special place because of Coach Frosty," I'm told by the team captain. "He emphasizes character, not winning. He wants us to have fun." Don't they say that about every football coach? And could they have come up with a more archetypal head baby-sitter for this trip than Coach Frosty Westering? Even the name is straight out of central casting. So is the jut-jawed, steely-eyed, gimpy-legged, crew-cut ex-Marine. The team hasn't brought cheerleaders with them, but they don't need any with Coach Frosty on board. Not only does he lead the squad in continual moronic cheers. Introduced as a world-renowned scribbler who is going to make them all instantly famous, I get a rendition of "Hey John! Go, John! Attaway! Attaway!" Coach Frosty barks out a steady stream of Pollyanna pep talks. "We've come to show these Chinese an upbeat way of life," he says, though I can't see how most Chinese will see anything but some kids trying as hard as they can to knock one another off their feet. "They have to beat us," he tells his squad of their opponents. "We just have to *be* us."

For thirty years, Frosty the Showman has been comfortable as a big fish in the small-college pond: winning championships at P.L.U. and inculcating in his charges "a quality education in a Christian context." There is nothing Christian about the way he barks out assignments for a mock game held on the greenest and most beautifully maintained soccer field in China. Doing his best impersonation of Bear Bryant, Coach Frosty waddles in knee-high tube socks and white Nikes with a limp that appears to be born of an old war wound. Behind his back, his boys have nicknamed him "Peg-Leg." At least a dozen geezers in short pants clutch clipboards and attend to every block and tackle of their charges. Frosty's main assistant is his earnest, blue-eyed son, Scott—what else?—an upstanding product of his father's system who was once drafted by the San Francisco 49ers.

The team has been brought to the practice facilities that ring the Olympic-quality stadiums constucted for the Asian Games. Just to their left, the Chinese Olympic Women's Softball squad is completing an impressive inning of fast-pitch. "Wow, I'd love to hand out scholarships to every one of these gals," I'm told by a salivating football assistant who doubles as Pacific Lutheran's baseball coach. He admits that he's had experience scouting the local populace as a former operative for the C.I.A. Shattering all stereotypes, not a one of the lanky Northern Ladies is under six feet—and these descendants of the Manchu tribes could beat the pants off the champs of any U.S. softball league. But while a few elite athletes in China have been trained in the arcane ways of baseball, somebody is going to have to do their best at explaining football. For that purpose, the team is accompanied by a college student named Yan I-Ming. Please call him "Mike." Spending a year at a junior college in Illinois has earned him the designation of "national expert" on American football—and the dubious distinction of having to do a play-by-play primer during the game. "Hey, Mike!" the Lutheran Lutes urge him on. "Go, Mike! Attaway! Attaway!"

Is this any way to have real contact with China? When this tour is over, the squads may still be able to say they've never left home. They are staying in the ultramodern, just completed wing of the Beijing Hotel, most of which is a musty Soviet-style monstrosity that may have more rooms and less charm than any other hotel on earth. They are loaded on and off tour buses for obligatory stops at the

Summer Palace and the Temple of Heaven. Like all honored "foreign experts," they are encouraged to part with their hard currency at colorless, state-run souvenir shops where surly attendants hawk silks, furs, obscure medicines made of antler powder. Do they have some ginseng concoction that will make a linebacker more ferocious? It's lucky the gang doesn't take note of the "Men's Cheerful Towel," a genital rub guaranteed to increase potency. At drab banquet pit stops, everyone passes on the quivering sea cucumbers but manages to use chopsticks to shovel down far oilier versions of sweet-sour dishes from home, washing it all down with dozens of Cokes. Later, when I explore some street stalls with a few of the Lutheran boys, I learn that they've been given extensive lectures about the dangers of diarrhea, that dread foe of the American way of life, able to fell strong fullbacks with a single swipe. Sneaking out of the hotel to wander among hygienic government-run food stalls, they won't even dare sample a spoonful of the blandest rice porridge.

It's not that these kids buy into accepting the official state version of things. It's just that they don't really know how or where to get off the tour. The staggering procession of gates, courtyards, and marble walkways in the Forbidden City at least affords the two squads a chance to fan out and mingle with the Chinese public. Uniformed schoolboys on class outings are frozen in awe at their first look at the massive African American lineman from Evangel. Not only have these boys never seen anyone that big or that dark, but they've surely never seen teenagers with single earrings dangling off their pointedly shaved heads. The interchange between little tyke and hunky athlete proceeds along rules that are universal, beyond cultures or words. The Chinese kids don't need to have collected bubble-gum cards to know that these Americans represent a style of brute force and controlled physicality that's far more casual, flashy, and egalitarian than that of their own kung fu masters. I doubt whether any of the football players learn much about the Ching Dynasty beyond what they've seen in Hollywood's "Last Emperor." They spend most of their time dashing from one stone dragon statuette to the next, posing before them by flexing their biceps or swooping up the nearest Chinese baby to cradle before the camera. The babies, too, have their skulls shaved for summer, tiny Emperors all. "We kicked a ball over the Great Wall," Coach Frosty boasts after the ultimate excursion. Of the Wall itself, he can only say, "Let me tell you, it left a profound impression." Exactly what sort of profundity he can't say.

China may have Chairman Mao, but America has Coach Frosty. Dozens of Coach Frosties, in fact, who are walking sets of motivational clichés: "Make the big time where you are!"..."Get out of the thermostat game, start playing the thermometer game!"..."Feedback is the breakfast of champions!" The language of teamwork is international, its ethic at once authoritarian and aimed at getting the maximum effort from every last foot soldier. Quarterback and Supreme Chairman alike get no crack at glory without anonymous grunts blocking up front. Keeping your eye on the goal post is always the aim. In politics, as in sports, a little simple-minded dedication goes a long way. In this way, Mao's cheerleading isn't that far removed from the sloganeering of Vince Lombardi. "Winning isn't everything, it's the only thing!" could have been the slogan of the Chinese Revolution. "Hold that line!" makes an even better cheer when applied to ideology.

*   *   *

"Just as there is not a single thing in the world without a dual nature, so imperialism and all reactionaries have a dual nature—they are real tigers and paper tigers at the same time."

Running Backs and Running Dogs

They say that sport is a universal language. But when it comes to China, everything gets lost in translation. Like the room service menus offering "Delicious Taste Beef Globules" and "Green Bean Juice." Like the suburban Beijing retreat that sought to entice tourists by calling itself the "Remote Place Hotel." Like the newly apolitical slogans everywhere exhorting the masses to "Merrily, merrily go to work. Safely, safely go home!" Once, at an outdoor market, I was served the most delicious tea, really an instant porridge made from almond paste, the water poured from a giant brass urn with two dragon-headed spouts. When I was dumb enough to inquire what the Chinese called their version of the samovar, the name was dutifully translated for me as, "Large brass urn with dragon-headed spout." China is maddeningly literal, so literal that meanings escape into nothingness. Everything is so uselessly obvious, so patently descriptive that words become cloaks of meanings as heavy as the green peacoats of People's Liberation Army sentries.

Hence the term "Oliveball"—in this case, a literal approximation that probably comes as close as any foreign culture can to a game that produces vocabulary like "flanker," "scrimmage," and "blitz." The irony is that while American football is one big groaning metaphor of imperialism in which faceless, helmeted drones bruise and bully their way into foreign territory, it has proved the American pop artifact most resistant to transplanting. While the era in which the Super Bowl and its militarist ethos has served as the highest expression of American jingoism, it is the more pastoral, nonterritorial pastime of baseball that our Marines have passed along through invasion and occupation. Even basketball has done better—embraced as the prime passion of Filipinos and Lithuanians alike. The recent "World Football League" has only underscored the absurdity of cheerleading squads in Frankfurt and

Barcelona. Only our protectorate of Guam has contributed a number of hyperthyroid cases with names so long they can't fit on their jerseys. In showing football to the Chinese, these teams are only showing up their own arrogance.

This "goodwill exchange" will engender good will solely because the government so declares. Never mind that the Chinese travel agencies have already turned a tidy profit by charging the players and their families $1,600 a head for the privilege of being good will ambassadors. Or that the Chinese have decided to charge up to 18 yuan (around $2.50) per ticket to the exhibition, virtually insuring that few common Chinese can afford to attend. Or that the Americans have barely set foot in China before they get involved in a rancorous dispute with Chinese officials. At the airport, the two local television news crews who had openly applied to travel with the teams have had all their cameras and equipment confiscated. It's not clear if the Chinese government really wants to control all coverage of the event—one would think they would benefit from the good publicity back in the States, but that would be too logical—or if some overzealous customs man has overstepped his bounds. It's one big bureaucratic "Catch 22": The journalists had been given permission to work as journalists but they cannot carry their gear so long as they are traveling with mere "tourist" visas. Rumors swirl that an official protest has been filed through the U.S. Embassy. At late-night negotiating sessions, college officials threaten to cancel the games unless the cameras are returned. But the rumors die quickly, the hollow threats fade. The news crews will never get their cameras out of hock, but the teams decide to play anyway.

Everything seems normal at the honorary banquet on the night before the game. Not "socialism with Chinese characteristics," as they used to say, but normal with Chinese characteristics—which means that most of the

Running Backs and Running Dogs

supposed honorees have to stand around in the atrium lobby of rose-colored marble while a bunch of aging bureaucrats and their mascara-masked wives toast one another smugly from the elitist dais. In this supposedly classless society, the VIPs sit and everyone else stands. So long as they can chow down on *chow mein*, none of the athletes or their few accompanying relatives complain or even notice how much they are treated as peons, shoulder-padded pawns. As in their dealing with the U.S. Congress over "Most Favored Nation" trading status, the Chinese have gambled that we need them more than they need us—and, once again, they have won.

"There is a Chinese saying, 'Either the East Wind prevails over the West Wind or the West Wind prevails over the East Wind.' I believe it is characteristic of the situation today that the East Wind is prevailing over the West Wind."

Game day at last, actually a muggy early summer late afternoon. The sky is as bleary gray as the low-lying, soot-encrusted *hutongs* that line the route to the stadium like a thousand indrawn peasant villages strung together to form a city. Inside their buses, the Lutes are getting pumped up. Even in the throes of culture shock, these kids can no longer squelch their fear of failure and/or glory. Now this is the version of sports I know and love: a bunch of brawny teenagers high on their own hormones, too naive to know better than to channel their aggressions toward whatever their trusted mentors point them. This time, impolite leers, sexist hoots greet People's Translator Number Seventeen Miss Wong, the only woman in sight, their surrogate cheerleader. The "Attaway" cheers rise and fall for nobody and nothing in particular. The linemen, already dressed for attack, are snarling and sneering. Miss Wong wants to know what they mean by the expression, "Game face." Once she gets the idea, she teaches them to say it in Chinese and the team chants the odd sounds over and over. The bus enters the stadium gates. An hour before kickoff, nobody is there but those in charge of security—which means the intimidating overkill of a few thousand soldiers, a couple of full battalions of armed ushers. "That's the marching band for you!" says one of the more irreverent Chinese guides with characteristic post-Tiananmen gallows humor.

The giant stadium is as modern as any in the West, empty now but for the lounging, smoking soldiers. The football field is perfectly laid out, the made-in-Taiwan goal posts of carefully measured width. The only thing wrong with this picture is that the billboards that line the outer track oval are all in black Chinese pictographs. A red banner has been hung underneath the press box, championing in blocky lettering something like, "The First China Exhibition Games American Sport Football!" Not so long ago, such a sign would have read, "Dig tunnels deep, store grain everywhere, and never seek hegemony!" Or, more likely, "People of the world, unite and defeat the U.S. aggressors and all their running dogs!" Now the running dogs are running backs.

Once upon a time in the East, these stands had been the site of the greatest flash-card displays in history, a hundred-thousand-strong section forming a giant portrait of the Great Helmsman, or the red flag, or a thousand socialist flowers in bloom. To try out their new "capitalist road," or to make the Americans feel at home, the Chinese have attempted a clumsy bit of Western commercialization. An English translation of one of the billboards explains that this game has been dubbed the first "Baolisha Cup"—after Baolisha, the brand name of a "Nonpoisonous Efficacious Commonly-Used Hygiean Insecticide." Not exactly the Super Bowl. But then, China is not exactly China anymore.

Running Backs and Running Dogs

This is just another town on a hot summer night with a lot of restless people hoping to find some distraction and an inkling of a better life. The old ways are more confusing than Confucian, the revolution repudiated, while the new-and-improved Western model is merely out for a test drive. Not so long ago, Beijing—doesn't the disused "Peking" now sound more exotic?—actually was "the other." Now China hardly knows what it is. There is nowhere in the world that is so much nowhere.

Though accustomed to their own peculiar brand of nowhere, the Lutes and the Crusaders might sense this if they ever took off their helmets. It's probably better for their sake that the kids are too wrapped up in their warmup calisthenics, hup-hup drills, glaring psych-out jobs on their opposite number, to notice that the only folks watching them are on assigned duty for the dreaded "Gong An" brain police. Slowly, a bit of the crowd begins to drift in. But this is hardly going to be the standing-room-only sell-out promised in the press releases. Apparently, the "work units" in which Chinese society is organized haven't been able to give away these expensive tickets, or order enough of their obedient cadre to make a show of filling the stands. The VIP boxes could actually use a few more Mao-suited bureaucrats. If any members of the Politburo are in attendance, I don't see them. The folks claiming the fifty-yard-line seats don't look decrepit enough to be of much import. Premier Li Peng, promised guest of honor, is a no-show. The so-called "butcher of Beijing" dares not show his face for long anywhere in China. In the end, a fairly young, nearly all male, chain-smoking contingent will more or less occupy the bottom tier of the stadium; perhaps thirty thousand or so, looking like fewer in the vast oval of seating, give or take much of the jaded Beijing press corps and all the U.S. Embassy employees it takes to unfurl one king-sized "Stars 'n' Stripes."

In the meantime, Coach Frosty has called a last team meeting. "Get those butterflies in formation!" he counsels the hyped-up charges who kneel in the grass all around him. This leader of men is resplendent in lumpy yellow sweat pants, his burr head glinting from the bank of stadium lights. He has last-minute announcements regarding defensive alignments, locker room facilities. "The toilet's a one-holer, so try to do your business now and move through quickly." Did Caesar not have to make similar prebattle remarks? "When you're on the field, you're a Lute," he reminds them. "And that makes you something extra special!" When you're a Lute, you're a Lute all the way! And I always thought it was a musical instrument. Then the squad heads to their assigned cubby under the stadium for a pregame prayer session. They link hands and bow heads while summoning the aid of the great flanker in the sky. To the Chinese who pass by, this curious ritual must look even stranger than the lighting of prayer incense and throwing of joss sticks. Why not, for the sake of true cultural exchange, call your plays with the *I Ching*?

Next comes the coin toss, the kickoff, the first grunts and surges at the line of scrimmage. The game itself resembles a glorified high school affair. Mr. Mike, the "foreign expert," tries his best to explain the rules as the game moves along. I wish I knew enough Chinese to gauge how misguided he may be. There is so much echo in the sound system that I'm not sure he's even being heard. Whenever there is a long run or a completed pass, a slow moan of collective astonishment rises from the back aisles. At frequent, inappropriate points, a section of fans stands in unison, trying to start a Western-style "wave" around the stadium. The wave never makes it to the shore. The biggest thrill comes when the Lutes and Crusaders on the bench turn their backs on the action and toss mini-sized footballs, donated by Coca-Cola, up into the stands. A similar uproar is occasioned at half time, when the players trot off the field close

Running Backs and Running Dogs

to the sidelines, giving "high fives" to the fans who reach over to touch the outstretched paws of the gladiators.

"What is the purpose?" one group of fans asks when I circulate in their midst. "I can't see anything in all this running into each other." The Chinese in attendance really do their best to get into the game. They truly want to find something in these repetitive pile-ups to be enthralled by. Lord knows, there is little enough enthralling in their daily lives. They are ready, eager, and willing to become true fans of almost anything we'd be willing to toss their way. They honestly want to be instructed in all the customary pleasures of the global monoculture, to finally "get it" when it comes to the twentieth century. But when it comes to second-division college football, I'm not sure that there is anything to get.

Here's my "extra point." Sport is sex in the open, the most interesting thing that we can do ensemble. And what links both activities is that they cannot take place outside a proper context. A specific sort of atmosphere is required for the successful completion of the act. We must agree upon a comon rulebook, know when to assess penalties, respond to the proper signals, understand why the whistle blows. And we must be aware of the degree of difficulty in order to exult properly when the ball splits the uprights. No marriage bed could be softer than the grass of our playing fields. Nothing is more loveless than a crowd that does not know when to cheer.

I cannot bear to stay until the end. So I have no report on how the young Lutes and Crusaders assessed their guinea pig status, their sweaty participation in what could be dubbed the world's first Fish Bowl. I know that Coach Frosty's troops have built an insurmountable lead, and that is enough for me. In my private scorekeeping, I take note of a more remarkable result. Tagging along on this most quintessentially American of events has caused not a whit of homesickness, backhanded pride, or identification.

John Krich

In that half-empty stadium, I accomplish my own "end-around." I have to admit, when I look at it straight-faced, that I understand less about my countrymen on the field—those wise-ass, rah-rah religious warriors, those sharp-talking, whistle-tooting inculcators of positive thinking—than I do about eternity's nameless masses in the stands. Given a choice, I would rather join these Confucianists for a post-game bowl of rice with a spicy dollop of Szechwan eggplant, perhaps a moldy dumpling or two, than sit at the bountiful training table of T-bones, nachos, stuffed potato skins. The Asian caution in the face of the terrors of the world, the dogged day-at-a-time scheming, the quietude that comes from keeping one's own counsel before stinging fate and the approbation of nosy neighbors, the love of the moderate path and the simple gesture well-achieved—these form a culture that I may view from afar but that I understand to my bones. Despite the passport I hold, the years of viewing half-time shows and Rose Bowl parades, I cannot as readily engage in the boundless, delusionary optimism of the world's Coach Frosties. In a way I could never have done when I was a self-proclaimed Maoist, a spoiled college brat exhorting my cohorts to take up the selfless, Spartan life, I have finally done it. With the help of football, I have crossed the goal line.

Born Nehmet Nusret in 1915 in Turkey, the author selected the name Aziz Nesin in 1933 when a Turkish law was passed requiring citizens to adopt surnames: He took his father's first name and chose "Nesin" ("What are you?" in Turkish) as his surname. After gaining an eclectic education under the supervision of various tutors and boarding schools, Mr. Nesin joined the army and simultaneously took up a literary career.

Mr. Nesin has written for a number of newspapers and magazines, using several pseudonyms. One of Turkey's great satirical humorists, he has written prolifically, producing pamphlets, essays, autobiographies, and novels—an average of one book for each year of his life. He spent a total of five and a half years in prison as a result of his writing.

The following short story is excerpted from his book *Rifat Bey Neden Kashiniyor*, published by Tekin Yayinevi, Istanbul.

Mr. Nesin lives in Istanbul, where he runs an orphanage and continues to write.

Lice Racing

"Have you ever seen a lice race?" I asked.

No, they never had. They had heard of lice racing, but had no idea what it was like; in fact, they didn't really believe there could be such a contest. They thought "lice racing" was colloquial for "making conversation."

"Did *you* ever see one?" they queried.

When I talk about lice races, I'm not just posing. I've seen lots of them. What's more, I've raced lice myself.

"How's it done? Tell us..."

"Well, one night near the end of the Second World War, I was drinking in a bar with friends. I must have let slip a few drunken remarks about the Prime Minister's government plan. (If I hadn't been drunk, would I ever have said anything? In about 20 years, the Prime Minister would probably have talked about his government plan anyway, so what was my hurry? That's drinking for you...) At any rate, sir, one of our loyal citizens in the bar scurried off to the police station and informed them that a man had said the workers must organize a union. On the basis of this incriminating information, five or ten plainclothes policemen entered the bar and surrounded me. We started talking and clinking glasses. Naturally, I didn't know they were political police. Up to that point, only my friends and I had been arguing; now, however, we were joined by these newcomers.

One of them said to me, "Our government's no good. What do you say?"

I told him, "You're right!"

We raised our glasses in a toast.

Another said, "The rich are exploiting the poor. Don't you agree?"

"Yes," I said.

Again we clinked glasses.

On my own, I said nothing; they spoke and I approved. But, truthfully, I was pleased and thought to myself, My word, the public is awakening; just listen to what these people are starting to think! But of course, these guys making me optimistic about the country were all police.

We left the bar together. I was staggering and was quite drunk, half from the drinks and half from joy. Three of the latecomers to the bar, with whom I had gotten on so well, held me tightly by the arms and walked me along.

When I said, "Don't bother, I can make it OK," they replied, "We can't do that, sir. We won't leave you until we get you to a safe place." My word, I thought, what decent people there are in this country, who, thank God, have drunk the milk of human kindness!

"With your permission, gentlemen, by God, I can make it."

"No, we definitely can't leave you. We'll take you."

Allah, Allah…They're taking me, but in the wrong direction.

"I live in Kasimpasha. Let me go, I can make it from here on my own. You've brought me this far. Thank you very much…"

"We can't leave you in the streets at midnight in this condition. You'll be our guest for tonight, at least."

What good-hearted people, my friends, God bless them! Transported by my high hopes for the country, reveling in my happiness, I sang softly.

"It's late, I don't want to be any trouble to you. With your permission…"

"God forbid. What trouble? We're doing our duty. Tonight you stay with us."

There were four of us, those three and me. We got into a car…and drove straight to the Istanbul Directorate of Security. But because I didn't know them I thought we were entering the apartment building where they lived.

"Oh, your apartment, how large!"

Lice Racing

We climbed the stairs. I kept thinking, I have to stay with these hospitable people, but how will I return their kindness in my little two-room bachelor pad? They still held my arms and took me up the stairs. At one point I said, "Friends, you do make me feel very ashamed."

In reply, the one on my left snapped, "Walk, you sonovabitch!" and when he elbowed me in the kidney, I collapsed on the steps.

No, just a coarse practical joke, maybe friendship, but I don't care for this kind of horsing around. They'd been so kind that I didn't suddenly get tough. After all, he said sonovabitch in fun, so, in order not to make a sharp retort, smiling at the remark as a joke, I said, "Come on, you bastards, don't do that..."

As soon as I said it, they began slapping, kicking, and pushing me around. After that, it was like a dream. I can't remember if I finally passed out from drunkenness or the beating. Early in the morning, I woke up to find I'd slept on the ice-cold stone floor. I tried to get up but couldn't even move, I was so pooped. I tried to collect my thoughts: I had made friends with some people at the bar the night before, then they took me with them as their guest. Good, but what kind of friendship was this?

Probably they were very drunk too...We got into a drunken argument. Now they'll awaken, offer their apologies, take me to breakfast...

Yes, I "breakfasted" on another beating as a suspect at the police station. From there to the prosecuting attorney's office, and then to the jail. By God! Nothing I'd said at the bar had anything to do with the current Prime Minister's announced government plan.

I ended up in prison. I had a few kurush* on me, but they soon melted away and I was stone-broke. No one visited, looked, or asked after me. They threw the penniless like me

---

*kurush—coin worth one hundredth of a Turkish pound, or lira.

into Father Adam, the hippie barracks. But if I start telling about the Father Adam Barracks, it'll take all night. Let me tell you just this much; maybe it will explain.

One day, before I had been assigned to the Father Adam Barracks, I and some other prisoners were walking in the central prison yard. Several convicts pressed against a window of the Father Adam Barracks kept yelling at a fellow prisoner walking in the yard, "Come on, man, you were just going to take a ten-minute walk, and it's been an hour already. Come on!"

Do you know why? In the big Father Adam Barracks all of the prisoners had to share one pair of trousers. Each one, in turn, put on this pair of pants and went out to sun himself in the yard. One of them had pulled on the pants an hour ago and not returned. The others couldn't go into the yard and grab him because they were dressed only in undershorts. They continued yelling through the barred window: "Man, won't you come back?—You'll come, whether you like it or not!"

Well, they threw me into the Father Adam Barracks. Every kind of poverty, outrage, imagined or unimaginable, was laid bare.

In those days, there was a typhus epidemic throughout Turkey. Even story-writer Kenan Hulülsi and novelist Iskender Fahrettin caught typhus and died. DDT hadn't yet been invented, and lice spread death.

Every morning when we got up, we found a number of prisoners dead from typhus. Their corpses were loaded onto stretchers and taken out to the yard. There wasn't a day without typhus deaths. Some days, as many as ten to fifteen people died. Typhus was a nasty disease; in the evening the patient's fever rose, by morning he was dead.

They put me in the Father Adam Barracks—rather, they shoved me in. I looked around; everyone in the barracks was piled one on top of the other, watching something. I squeezed in and looked, but didn't understand. I asked

Lice Racing

someone, "What's going on, friend?"

"Lice racing."

What! Lice racing? My God, people are dying of typhus and they're racing lice in here!

The men in this barracks are accursed, stubborn people; it doesn't do any good to say anything to them. As if my eyes could speak, I looked at one of them and tried to convey my message about the danger of death from lice. A man with a long beard, clad in long, gray, dirty undershorts, told me, "These lice were raised specially for racing; they can't have any germs."

"How do you know they're germ-free?"

"They're not in contact with other lice. They're given special care, nourishment, and training."

Now let me tell you about lice racing. The racetrack is nice and smooth. They spread a dirty cloth on the floor and place a large tin can on top of it. A circle is drawn with chalk around the base of the can and the can removed. Outside this circle, a much larger circle is drawn. All the racing lice are placed in the inner circle. Naturally the lice begin to walk. The louse that crosses the outer circle first wins first place; after him come second and third.

Just like when they gamble in other barracks, in lice racing there's someone in charge of the pot. This "banker," who is also barracks boss, acts as referee. He decides how the lice place; no one can oppose him.

Everyone in the barracks who wants can enter his louse in the race. But to enter, it's necessary to put up money in advance, let's say three lira for each louse. If ten lice race, there's thirty lira in the pot. The owner of the louse that comes in first gets one third of the pot, or ten lira. The owner of the louse coming in second gets double the money he put in, that is, six lira. The owner of the louse placing third gets one-and-a-half times the money he put in, that is, four-and-one-half lira. The owner of the louse coming in fourth gets his money back, that is, three lira.

Everything else goes to the barracks boss.

Those without enough money to enter lice in the race make bets of twenty-five or fifty kurush. Those with no money at all bet their daily bread ration. The banker takes ten percent from the winners. The barracks sweeper collects both the money and the bread rations.

The boss was called Dirty Süleyman. He had used a knife on his own mother, received a long sentence, and thus was called Dirty Süleyman. He owned and raced lice also.

When I first entered the barracks, a race was almost over. It ended and the winners collected their money, the banker his cut. Those who lost cursed their lice. The sweeper removed the can and the dirty cloth on which the race was held. Only then did they notice that a new man had come to the barracks. To every, "Good luck, friend," I replied, "So be it, thanks, comrade."

Soon, when everyone in the barracks had withdrawn into his own world, a man with his left eye shrunken to the size of a chickpea approached me and started talking. Later I learned that he was a nutty Jew called Marshal David. He got his name from wearing medals and decorations on his chest when he was on the outside. When he entered prison, they ripped off all his medals and decorations. But, because Marshal David couldn't carry on without medals and decorations, he fastened pop-bottle caps, bottle corks tied with string, wood chips, and buttons onto the chest of his dirty, ragged shirt. Marshal David was a graverobber who unearthed corpses. One night, carrying off a coffin with a newly buried corpse, he was caught. They hauled him off to prison.

Marshal David bragged that there was no better louse trainer in the entire world than he. If there were a lice racing competition at the Olympics and David could get his louse into it, his louse would win the gold medal.

"In that case, you must win all the races here," I said.

Lice Racing

"No."

"Why not, then?"

"There's a reason, but I can't say."

Suddenly he asked me, "Do you have lice?"

When I didn't answer, he repeated his question: "Do you have lice—in your underwear?"

"I don't think so, because a few days ago, in the quarantine barracks, they gave us baths and put our clothes through the sterilizer."

This pleased Marshal David. "In that case, you're clean. Will you be partners with me in lice racing?"

"I don't know; how's it played?"

"I'll teach you. Be partners with me, do whatever I say, and you'll see; my louse will win all the races tonight."

While he was talking like that, the sweeper spread out the cloth, set up the can, and carefully drew two circles with chalk.

Marshal David told me, "Come on, put up three lira for the two of us; we'll win, you'll see."

"I don't have three lira."

David was very disappointed. But I really didn't have three lira; my personal wealth amounted to one-and-a-half, and I was afraid to spend that.

Excitedly, he urged, "We'll win, come on, we'll win!"

"I'm broke."

"Aren't you wearing something you can sell?"

"You can see I don't have a thing, I'm flat broke."

He spotted the fountain pen in my pocket.

"Shall we sell the pen?"

I gave him the pen. He called through the window to someone in the yard, then threw it to him. Soon it was sold for a lira. The man outside pushed a lira under the barracks' iron door. I became interested. I handed David my scarf, and it sold for two-and-a-half lira.

Then, saying, "Come here!" he pulled me into the corner of the barracks, raised his arm, and untied a dirty cloth

103

from a place near his armpit. From the wool beneath the cloth, he drew out a louse, an enormous louse.

"This here's Majar,* my Hungarian. I named him Majar because he's as big as a horse. You've got to be able to recognize this louse. I'll paint Majar so you can tell him from the other lice."

He stuck a pin in his hand and painted Majar's back red with the blood.

"Now you'll know him," he said. "Look, open your ears and listen carefully. Majar's coming in first is in your hands. As soon as the lice cross the first line, your eyes will be on our Majar. Whatever side you stand on, Majar will run toward you. If you see another louse move ahead of Majar, then move to the other side so Majar will run to you. Understand?"

"I don't understand."

"Hey Allah! I'm forced to reveal my secret. Friend, these lice love cleanliness. They quickly pick up the scent of humans, fleeing from dirty people and running toward clean ones. Everyone believes that lice enjoy filth. No, they love cleanliness. Throw a single louse among a thousand people, he goes, searches, and finds the one who is clean. You get the trick? Right now, there's no one in this barracks cleaner than you. Whatever side you stand on, Majar will run that way. But the poor fellow's aging. If you see another louse passing our Majar, he's also running toward you; so run to the side that Majar's close to so he'll come in first."

The sweeper shouted, "Come to the races! Come on, the races!"

We shelled out our three lira. Twelve lice were entered in the race. At the boss's signal, the twelve were placed in the small inner circle. Each louse owner, or those who'd bet on his louse, yelled its name as loud as they could. Like race-

---

*majar—Turkish word for Hungarian; slang for louse.

Lice Racing

horses, every racing louse had a name and everyone recognized his own louse.

"Come on, Pheasant!"

"Fly now, Cow!"

"Hang in there, Sprite, my girl!"

"Fly, Seagull, fly! Please fly, Seagull!"

"Come on, you damn thoroughbred native; go, man!"

My eyes were on our Majar. I had recognized him at once from the blood on his back.

At first, the lice in the inner circle stood there confused. They stirred, then stopped again. One of them rushed in my direction. Pushing me, Marshal David said, "Go to the other side!"

I changed position. When I changed places, the louse in front stopped; he turned this way and that, as if searching for someone. Again he raced toward me.

My eyes were on Majar. He, too, was coming toward me, but in fourth place. I moved to the side closest to him. This time Majar was in front, about to reach the outer circle. Just then, an amazingly quick louse caught up with Majar, and I slipped to the left. When I slipped to the left, the louse in the lead became confused and stopped. David yelled at the top of his voice, "Come on, tiger! Majar!"

"Pheasant, my boy!"

All the racing lice fanned toward me like iron filings toward a magnet. But in front was our bloodied Majar...Majar came in first, and they gave us eighteen lira, half the thirty-six-lira pot.

We started the second race. This time fourteen lice were entered. Again Majar took first place.

The lice races continued throughout the night. Majar won more than a hundred lira. Near morning, the races ended. Everyone picked up his louse, put him in a nest of wool wrapped in cloth and secured him to his armpit. The race lice were nourished between wool and oily skin.

Marshal David and I divided the money. He said,

"Didn't I tell you? There's no louse trainer better than me. I know the louse's psychology. Just be careful not to get dirty."

We won money at the lice races every day. A heroin addict, David was using lots of it now that he had the money.

The thing that really amazed me was that somehow these naked men in Father Adam Barracks were finding the money for lice racing. It seemed as if this barracks was a mint.

By my fourth day there, the lice didn't come toward me as fast as they used to. Marshal David said, "Finally, you too are getting dirty."

They still came toward me, though very slowly. Dirty Süleyman was getting very upset at Majar's winning every time. There were louse sales as well as races in the barracks. Fast lice brought high prices.

Dirty Süleyman said, "Hey, David, sell me this Majar."

"All right, I'll sell him, brother."

They entered into some tight haggling. After dickering hard, they agreed on fifty lira. Dirty Süleyman counted out the fifty and took Majar. Being a boss, he didn't feed his racing lice himself but had the sweeper or one of the boys do it. The sweeper took Majar and carefully settled him in the wool under his armpit.

Marshal David told me, "We've got a new trick; this time Majar will no longer come in first. Look, I'll tell you what to do. You'll no long stand on the side but lean over the lines from above. Understand? The lice will get your scent and won't be able to go in any direction."

The race started. This time Marshal David entered another louse, named Greyhound.

I leaned over, watching the race from above. The lice stayed in the inner circle. They continually stirred because they wanted to come to me, but not having wings they couldn't fly. Majar, especially, was rotating around his

Lice Racing

rump. The other lice finally left the inner circle, crawling slowly. Majar didn't even leave the inner circle.

Dirty Süleyman nearly went mad with rage.

"Come on, Majar, damn Majar...Run, you low-down, despicable!" he kept screaming.

That day there were four races, and in all four Majar didn't even make it out of the inner circle. Dirty Süleyman went crazy and flattened Majar with his fingernail.

Marshal David, who was very mournful after this crime, said to me, "The animal's blood is on our hands."

"Very well, why didn't he move, David?"

"Well, why would he move? You saw his belly, how swollen it was. He couldn't carry his belly. One must leave the louse hungry before a race. I fed Majar well. You leaned over, the animal struggled, couldn't fly. His stomach was swollen, he couldn't walk...He's gone, our Majar."

From that day on, the old excitement was gone from lice racing. The lice no longer raced toward me as they used to—I had become as dirty as they were.

Translated from the Turkish by
Joseph and Viola Jacobson

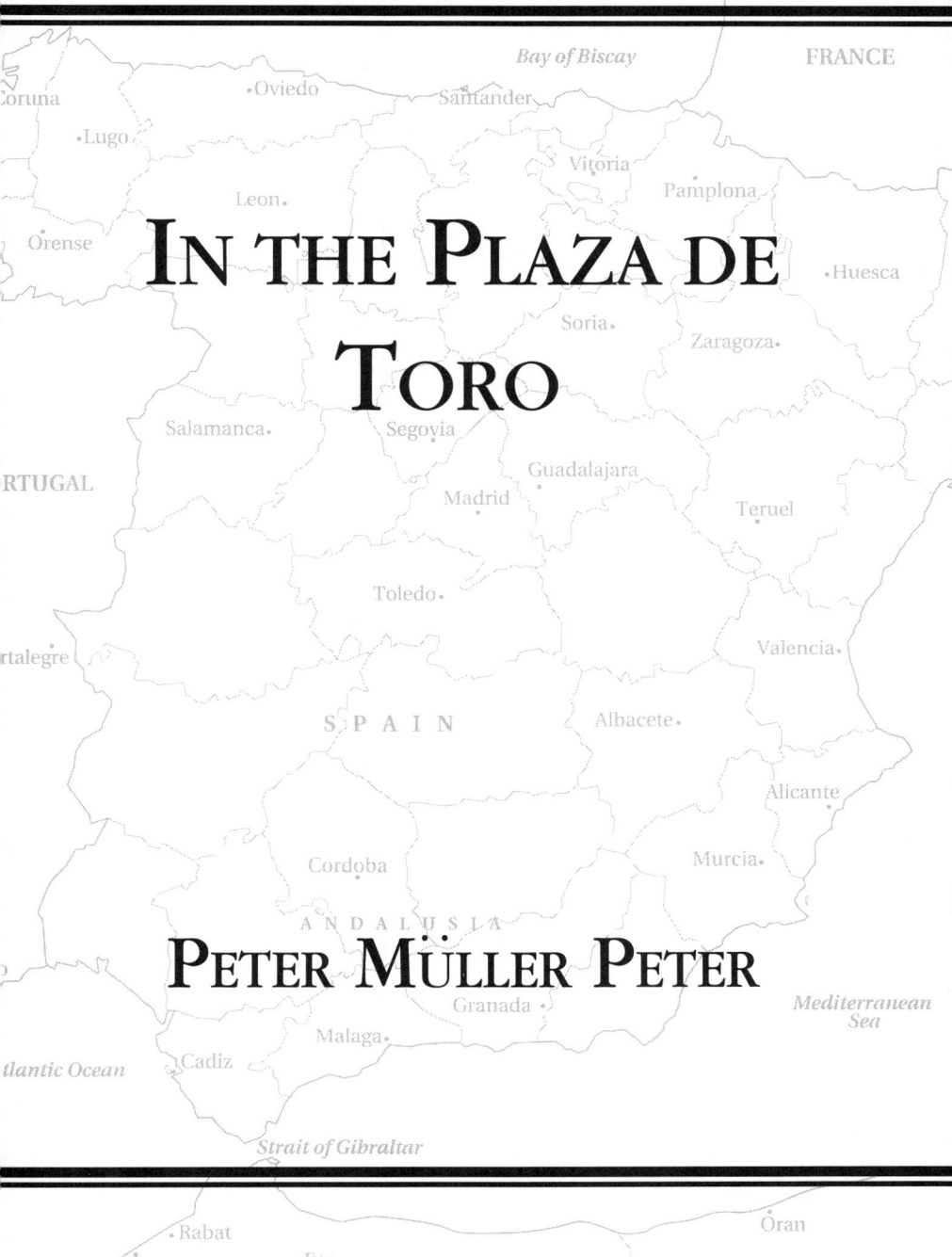

In the Plaza de Toro

Peter Müller Peter

Peter Müller Peter was born in Peru in 1953. He completed his studies in architecture and fine arts at the University of Zurich, Switzerland.

Mr. Müller is a commercial free-lance photographer who has worked on major advertising campaigns, including Coca-Cola, Iberia, Tourismo de España, and De Beers. In addition, he was photography assistant and camera technician, respectively, for renowned photographers Bert Stern and Eddie Vorkapich. While working on an advertising brochure for a convention facility on the grounds of a bull-breeding ranch in Andalusia, he became acquainted with the people, bulls, and horses involved in bullfighting. He spent much of the next four years on the ranch. He subsequently published a book about bullfighting, *España por Dentro*, for which he recently received an honorable mention from the European Art Directors Club.

The photographs that accompany the following essay are drawn from *España por Dentro*.

Mr. Müller has been working out of his studio in Madrid since 1980.

In the Plaza de Toro

Bullfighting expresses a particularly Spanish fascination with machismo. For the *rejoneador* or *torero*, bullfighting is almost a vocation, a religion, a fatal ballet where the dancer daily perfects his discipline, regularly risks his life in the arena. In the choreography of horse, bull, and man, one encounters the nobility of a culture formed over many centuries and rooted in the countryside of Andalusia. It is not a sport that can be hurried. Talent is required, patient discipline is its necessary taskmaster. One trains a bull for five years for the sake of ten minutes in the arena. It is the challenge of the bullfighter to demonstrate that he is braver than a bull.

In Spain, bullfighting was first practiced on horseback. Mounted soldiers who fought wars between the Moors and the Christians would train and exhibit their bravery by spearing bulls. This form of bullfighting was so popular, in fact, that in the sixteenth century Pope Sixtus V forbade the clergy to attend bullfights. That prohibition was later rescinded.

The practice of bullfighting gradually became fashionable among the nobility of Spain who were able to afford the horses, the bulls, and a private arena in which to hold the contests. By the beginning of the eighteenth century, Spanish landowners on horseback were regularly challenging bulls with spears to demonstrate their courage. These were the first *rejoneadores*, so called because of their *rejóns*, the lance-like sticks that they used to kill the bull. Approximately five feet in length, the *rejóns* were tipped with an almond-shaped blade six inches long and two inches wide.

The *rejoneadores* were assisted in the ring by peasants, who were on foot. The peasants helped maneuver the bull in the arena with a colorful cape, assisted fallen riders, and used a sword to deal the fatal blow to wounded bulls too difficult to kill from horseback. The peasants soon became popular performers in their own right. These were the original *toreros*, bullfighters who challenged the bulls with cape and sword and without the benefit of a horse. While the gentlemanly art of bullfighting on horseback *(rejoneo)* remained the exclusive province of the wealthy, this new form of bullfighting on foot *(toreo)* now opened up participation to the poor of Spain.

As bullfighting became increasingly popular, the location of the fights shifted to the plazas of cities. This allowed those who lived around the square to observe the spectacle from their windows—but few others. Soon, construction of *plazas de toro* or bullfighting arenas began in cities, allowing large crowds to attend the fights. Rules were regularized for *rejoneo* and *toreo*. Cattle owners bred bulls specifically for fighting, breeding them for size, speed, and courage.

Several centuries earlier, the Cartujanos, an order of Spanish monks, had begun breeding horses for use by officers in the battlefield. They were bred for bravery, physical beauty, and responsiveness to their rider, and trained to execute martial moves in the midst of battle. In peacetime, this equestrian training continued, known as dressage. Later, when *rejoneo* grew popular, the same breeds used for dressage were trained for the bullfighting arena.

In the 18th century, many aspects of *toreo* were developed and refined, including the basic pass with the cape, or *Verónica*; the wearing of an elegant, beautifully embroidered costume; and the creation of teams of bullfighters, or *cuadrillas*. In addition, the participation of the *picador* became a regular part of *toreo*. A mounted assistant to the *torero*, the *picador* thrusts a lance between the shoulders of the bull. This focuses the bull's attention on the *torero*, encouraging it to attack and causing it to lower its head. The animals stand so tall that it would be virtually impossible for a *torero* to fight a bull with its head up. A bull's horns

are like knives, nineteen inches in circumference. A mature bull weighs approximately 1,000 pounds.

In the 1920s, *rejoneo*, too, underwent transformation. It became stylized, involving half-turns and sidewise passes of the horse. In the 1940s, Alvaro Domecq y Díez refined it further, copying as many of the *torero* moves as possible and making *rejoneo* a more daring, dignified, and elegant performance. His son, Alvaro Domecq y Romero, followed in his footsteps and built upon his work, and in 1973 founded the Royal Andalusian School of Equestrian Art. In turn, the nephews of Alvaro Domecq y Romero are both *rejoneadores*.

Bulls are kept in large spacious fields, separate from the cows. They are generally peaceful when within the group

and do not like to be separated from it. When the bulls are two years old, two men with lances ride horses into the field to test the young bulls, or *novillos*. Each lance has a short iron tip, just over an inch in length, to prevent serious injury to the calf. The *novillos* are collected in a corral at one end of the field and are let one at a time into the field. The *novillo* sprints to its favorite section of the field and is followed by the two lancers, who flank it on either side. On cue, the lancer on the left rides quickly forward and then abruptly to the right, causing the *novillo* to turn; the second lancer throws his lance into the right hindquarter of the *novillo*. These sudden moves cause the *novillo* to stumble and somersault. When it gets up, it turns and attacks the horses. At that moment, its courage is proven. From that day forward, the *novillo* is groomed for bullfighting in the plaza. For the next three years, it is well fed, well cared for, trained, and kept from contact with the cows. When it is five years old, it is taken to the arena.

The two-year-old cows are tested as well. If a cow proves courageous, it is kept for breeding. In this way, only the best animals are allowed to breed and to fight in the plaza.

Horses, too, are carefully trained for *rejoneo*. Two breeds predominate, Andalusian and Arabian. For four years a *rejoneador* teaches his horses obedience and the stylized movements of the arena. Horse and rider become sensitive to each other, moving flawlessly in tandem. The horses learn to use their tails in the same way *toreros* use their capes and to execute maneuvers gracefully.

In their fifth year, the horses are acquainted with the power and speed of the bulls. A *rejoneador* rides his horse, draped in a leather apron, into the bull field and provokes a bull. If the horse does not move quickly enough when the bull charges, the horse is attacked but is protected by the apron. In this way, the horse learns to respect the bull. Over the course of a year, it will become adept at maneuvering around its formidable opponent.

When tourism began to boom in Spain, the nature of bullfighting changed. Previously, bullfights had been held only in large cities, since a mature bull needs an immense arena in which to run. With the influx of tourists, bastardized versions began to appear elsewhere.

Many tourists had heard of the bullfights in Madrid or Seville but did not want to visit cities preferring instead to

see the pueblos of southern Spain. Pueblo dwellers soon perceived the tourists' desire to see a bullfight, and they started constructing diminutive *plazas de toro*, too small for a mature bull. Rather than investing in a five-year-old bull, which costs roughly $10,000, they would buy a *novillo*. Since a professional *torero* or *rejoneador* would not fight an immature bull in an undersized arena, poor bullfighters fought the *novillos*. Predictably, the bullfighting in these little plazas was not done properly. This unfortunate practice continues.

Consequently, when tourists visit Spain, many end up watching "bullfights" in a small Andalusian pueblo. What they see is a poor imitation. They do not see the art or skill, a properly trained bull or disciplined bullfighter, the respect that a serious bullfighter has for a mature bull, a genuine bullfight. They do not have the opportunity to be awed by the fact that a man can stand in front of an animal that weighs half a ton and challenge it to a fight. They see only a bloody, brutal display. This is the erroneous impression of Spanish bullfighting that many tourists carry away.

The most important *plazas de toro* in Spain are in Madrid,

Seville, and Malaga. No dedicated bullfighter would fight in a plaza where he cannot fight, where a fine bull cannot run.

As in the past, *rejoneadores* usually come from wealthy families. To bullfight on horseback, one needs to be well-heeled, since horses are expensive and a *rejoneador* needs at least five of them. He takes a few rounds with one horse, returns to the corral for another, and comes out again. Each of his horses has been trained to perform a special role during the bullfight, and the *rejoneador* wants to exhibit those abilities in the arena. The *rejoneadores* often possess a private plaza where they train.

Likewise, the *toreros* usually come from poorer families and are not well educated. They are introduced to *toreo* by a bull breeder, who allows the boys from the pueblo to come

to his private arena and use a cape to try two or three rounds on foot with a young bull. This allows the bull breeder to observe how his bulls move in the ring. In addition, when he spots a potential *torero,* he recommends him to a manager. If the manager accepts the young man into his stable, he supports him and gains exclusive right over everything he does in connection with bullfighting. The manager provides his aspiring bullfighters, called *maletillas,* with attire, food, lodging, and training.

Rejoneadores and *toreros* alike begin training when they are about nine years old. A skilled *rejoneador* or *torero* earns $40,000 for each *corrida* in which he participates. A *corrida* is a series of six bullfights in which three (sometimes fewer) bullfighters participate, each engaging in at least two bull-

fights; a *rejoneador* fights in a *corrida de rejoneo*, a *torero* in a *corrida de toro*. A popular bullfighter can be involved in as many as seventy to eighty *corridas* a year. *Rejoneadores* and *toreros* who have been successful often become bull breeders.

Rejoneadores and *toreros* are pop idols, known for their bravery and machismo. They are particularly popular among women. Their movements are graceful. Their culture is sexy, narcissistic, and disciplined.

All of it—the bullfighters' sequined costume, the trappings of the horses, the architecture of the bull rings, the rituals—is one with the Andalusian soul, capable of confronting the moment at once with extroversion and reservation, bravely and fearfully, abruptly and politely. The bull first lives surrounded by the silent countryside, a world that offers few opportunities to be seen, then faces another that arrogantly exposes itself, the bull ring. Before this world of gold and sequins, brass bands and kerchiefs, with blood and shouts, stands the bull and death. An enthralling world, in which predjudice is rampant, and which one has to penetrate deep to gain even the slightest acquaintence. But that is another story.

THE SOCIALIST SPORTS PROGRAM

BRIGITTE BERENDONK

Brigitte Berendonk was born in 1942 in Dankmarshausen, in what later became East Germany. As a teenager, she began to distinguish herself as a top athlete in track and field. Among her many accomplishments, she was German youth champion in the pentathlon, first in the German Democratic Republic (GDR) and then, after her family defected, in the Federal Republic of Germany (FRG); FRG champion in discus and shotput; two-time participant and finalist in the Olympics; winner of the silver medal at two student world championships; and elected speaker of the FRG women's track-and-field team.

When still an athlete, Ms. Berendonk recognized the destructive effect of androgenic-anabolic steroid use in sports. When East Germany fell, she began a rigorous investigation of formerly classified documents to determine the extent of the drug program and the government's involvement in it. The following selection is an excerpt from the book she wrote on the basis of her inquiry, *Doping Dokumente: Von der Forschung zum Betrug*.

Ms. Berendonk teaches high school English and physical education. She and her husband, Dr. Werner Franke, live in Heidelberg, Germany.

The Socialist Sports Program

In the following excerpt, one-time East German swimming coach Michael Regner reports the program of giving androgenic anabolic steroids to swimmers on the national team. Regner's statements have been substantially confirmed by numerous uncovered official documents, public confessions, and testimonies from doctors and scientists of the former East German state, the German Democratic Republic (GDR), which collapsed in 1990.

I worked for eleven years at a military sports club (ASK) and had rapid success as a coach, first as a sports official at a political youth organization *(Pioniereinheit)* in Havelberg, and later, beginning in December 1978, at a military sports club in Potsdam. There I worked with a group of twelve-year-old boys, who soon won their first championship at the "Youth Games of Friendship." I was fortunate enough to be able to reinspire athletes who, according to general opinion, had already peaked in athletic ability and development. In short, I fulfilled the "plan" in every situation.

The day came unexpectedly, at least that is how it seems to me now, when I was accepted as a full member of the national sports system of the German Democratic Republic (GDR), which also meant that I was fully initiated into its deeper secrets. Everything happened so casually and naturally that, at first, I did not recognize anything particularly unusual.

At the time, June 1987, I was responsible for a group of twelve- to thirteen-year-old female swimmers. Among them I discovered two girls with exceptional talent: Grit Müller (who eventually won the silver medal as a member of the East German team in the 800-meter freestyle at the 1991 World Swimming Championships in Perth, Australia) and Diana Block. Both swimmers were only thirteen years old at the time but already swam so fast that they were scheduled to be in the starting heat at the European Youth Championships in Rome.

One particular day, I was standing at the edge of the pool during training as usual when Dr. Jochen Neubauer, designated by the Potsdam ASK as physician for the swim team, called me into his office, room 131, at the front of the swimming center. Dr. Neubauer closed the door behind him, and we sat across from each other at a small conference table. "Pay close attention," he said. "There are some pills in here. Do not ever talk about this, and give one-half tablet per day to those athletes who will be traveling to the European Championships. You will soon see that this is the right thing to do."

There were twelve blue tablets in the envelope he handed me, each round and about four millimeters in diameter. I was to administer one-half tablet to each of the swimmers over the next twelve days "in a way that they will not notice," as Dr. Neubauer stressed. For simplicity's sake, Neubauer suggested that I dissolve the pills in water and then "mix them into a vitamin drink." When I asked him directly what kind of pills they were, Dr. Neubauer responded curtly, "I will explain that to you another time. Just do it. Everything will be all right."

Finally, he explained some possible side effects: The girls, he commented, would probably "become a little funny" because of the pills.* If an athlete were to "complain of muscle tension," I was supposed to suspend a "dose" for one day. Due to our relationship of absolute mutual trust at the time, I did not ask any further questions and followed his directions strictly.

---

* Author's note: This cynical tone plays on the fact that when thirteen-year-old girls receive androgenic anabolic steroids, early blooming of sexual libido might have to be reckoned with. It was expected that this could eventually lead to some "funny" situations, for the girls as well as for the trainers.

The Socialist Sports Program

I always prepared a daily vitamin mixture that included glucose, citrus, and occasionally iron and potassium-magnesium for my athletes. I would pour the mixture into plastic bottles labeled with a name-tag. During training breaks, the girls would drink from them. Grit Müller and Diana Block subsequently swallowed one-half of a blue tablet daily during the next twelve days—without their knowledge.

Both girls proceeded to complete an incredible session. They swam their laps, climbed out of the pool, and were rejuvenated so quickly that they could have immediately conquered another series with ease. At the time, I attributed the increase in their endurance to the inspiration of the upcoming European Youth Championships, which seemed to be an invigorating and motivating factor.

As I reflect on this today, I must reproach myself at how boundlessly naive I was. I justified it at the time by the thought that the girls received such a vast quantity of pill-mixtures anyway that just one more couldn't possibly do any harm. Today I know, however, that this was just a partial truth.

When I began mixing the new kind of pill into the plastic bottles, I began to dope them, without their or my own knowledge. I administered an androgenic-anabolic steroid called Oral-Turinabol.

At the time, I thought it inconceivable that such drugs could be used in GDR sports. For years I had believed in the fundamental goodness of socialism. I was a devout Communist. My friends had always commented that I was the type of person who would stand on the highest mountain and wave the red flag. I believed in the Party, the State, and our German Socialist society. For this reason, I was fascinated by competitive sports. It was an area of absolute strength, of honesty, a domain in which socialism had continuously proven to be the better system.

The girls' achievements in Rome further strengthened

this mistaken belief. Grit Müller won the 800-meter freestyle event. Two days earlier, she had completed two difficult events, the 400-meter freestyle and the 400-meter medley, at intervals of approximately 40 minutes, for which she had received the bronze medal. Such achievements—which I see now through the lens of my current perspective—are attributable almost exclusively to the use of anabolic steroids. The athletes were just as oblivious as I was at the time. In their minds, doping existed only in other countries, capitalist countries.

Later, we had to prepare the athletes for the moment when they would possibly have to undergo drug inspections at upcoming international competitions. This problem was resolved in typical, hypocritical GDR fashion.

During the European championships in Rome, Wolfram Allendorf, team leader at the time, gave the gathered troops "verbal guidance." "Okay, be careful," Mr. Allendorf declared. "It is proper to say that we find ourselves here on enemy territory. The capitalists want to find fault with socialist sports." According to Mr. Allendorf, the most dangerous aspect was "the regulation of performance-enhancing drugs in capitalist countries. In order to find us guilty, they try to fill our vitamin bottles secretly with illicit drugs." Therefore, each athlete was to keep close watch over his or her bottle, so that it would never stand unobserved. In truth, however, over the past two years, no one had ever been caught, precisely because the anabolic steroids were administered under such a well-devised system. Unfortunately, I realized this only later.

I had my next private meeting with Dr. Neubauer at the end of September 1987. He invited me into his office again. He laid a form on the table. The doctor stated that I must have noticed the fact "that we do certain things that are never to be brought to the attention of the public eye." Now that I had become an important figure in the sports plan of the club, the doctor said he would, "request my

The Socialist Sports Program

signature on the document in front of me. I would receive any follow-up information from [him] later."

The gist of the form in front of me was as follows: With this document, the undersigned is made aware of the fact that all actions pertaining to "supporting substances"* are to be kept under the strictest pledge of secrecy. Any contravention of this secret oath will be punished.

I expressed curiosity about the meaning of "supporting substances," but I did not receive an answer. However, I signed the document immediately because I really did want to continue working at the highest level of competitive sports. The conversation had lasted less than ten minutes. Four weeks later Dr. Neubauer did explain the concept of supporting substances. According to him, it was merely "a medical contribution to help the athletes endure more pressure and physical exertion and to loosen them up a bit more psychologically."

At the end of October I was offered the coaching position for the leading group of female athletes in the Potsdam ASK. Aside from Grit Müller and Diana Block, Katrin Gronau, Heide Grün, Corinna Meyer, Franziska Zietermann, and Andrea Koch belonged to this elite team. I was now responsible for giving as many of these athletes as possible the opportunity to participate in the 1988 Olympic Games in Seoul. The European Cup in Monte Carlo, December 12-13, 1987, was on the program as the first serious test of the entire plan.

In preparation for these events, as relayed to me by Dr. Neubauer, a so-called "cycle" was to be carried out. The cycle called for the administration of supporting substances to the athletes over a period of twelve days.

For the first time, I did not receive the tablets in an envelope but in their original packaging. The doctor subsequently

---

*supporting substances—In the GDR, this was the official code term for performance-enhancing drugs, usually androgenic-anabolic steroids.

ordered me to remove the pills from their protective covering and then to destroy the foil completely, together with all other left-over packaging. This was to be done "in a manner that no one will notice."

I thus removed the pills from the foil behind the closed door of the training room, took the waste home with me and burned it in the oven. Even my wife took no notice of my action. It remained a matter between myself and the doctor.

I abruptly found myself situated between a rock and a hard place: On the one hand I knew that the GDR's motto in support of a "clean" athletic program had turned out to be a farce. On the other hand, I was now somewhat a part of the secret plan. I had slipped unexpectedly into the role of accomplice.

Against my better judgment, I spoke to my athletes concerning these "actions within sports medicine" and informed them that there would be "no disadvantages whatsoever." I insisted that if they "wanted to beat the others, there [was] nothing for [them] to do other than to participate." I then sent the girls, on an individual basis, to the doctor. Even they had to sign the pledge that swore them to secrecy. They were not even allowed to discuss the situation with their parents.

I viewed such practices as definitely "unclean" but maintained a clear conscience about it. I was thoroughly convinced that capitalism was geared solely for the destruction of our socialist system. In order to prevent this, I thought, all methods or substances must be allowed. In addition, the doctor assured me, "Everybody [is] doing it anyway, including sports programs in the West. Only we do it a little better."

In fact, I subsequently observed the coaches of the male athletic teams, Jürgen Hoefner and Lutz Wanja, leaving the doctor's office with packages of the same medication I had received. Short visits to room 131 were, from that

The Socialist Sports Program

point on, a matter of course. Whenever a "cycle" began, we were called in and given "the stuff."

Older athletes were used to the administration of anabolic steroids as part of the daily routine. Sometimes the pills were even referred to in jest. For instance, if someone in the weight room, be it a track and field athlete, a canoe racer, or a gymnast, reached the maximum weight level, comments such as the following made the rounds: "So, you've thrown in three blues again, huh?" or "He's obviously devoured too much 'crystal.'" On the other hand, the era in which East German athletes were fed drugs by the spoonful and girls were running around with baritone voices was already history.

The administration of androgenic-anabolic steroids was centrally controlled. A committee in East Berlin drew up a "Plan for Studies in Sports Medicine" every year. This served no other purpose than to build up the athletes systematically through the use of anabolic steroids.

Such programs laid out in great detail which athlete in which club was to take supporting substances and at what time. Only the dosage was determined on the spot. At the end of the year, the bosses of the Sports Medicine Service in Berlin were told how many tablets each athlete had taken during the past twelve months; coaches were obliged to keep track of each cycle in a very precise protocol.

The Committee on Sports Medicine then sent their up-to-date plans to the doctors at the various clubs, and physicians informed the coaches. During our conversations, Dr. Neubauer usually had a folder with the drug schedules for all my athletes lying in front of him. His "requests" were always fulfilled very carefully because they guaranteed perfect training and success. No member of the Potsdam ASK was ever convicted of doping.

In order to close out the possibility of danger completely, no athlete who had not undergone a drug test ahead of time was allowed to leave the country. The "Central Drug

Control Laboratory of Sports Medicine" in Kreischa had been given the responsibility of testing.

Every one-week period before travel to a competition in another country, athletes of the Potsdam ASK were required to convene in the club at six o'clock in the morning to turn in a urine sample. Regularly between six and six-thirty an official car drove up, collected the samples, and drove immediately back to Kreischa. A few days later the club's doctor would receive the results over the telephone.

I experienced only one instance in which a positive analysis was given. During a training session at a camp in Lindow, we were told that one of the young swimmers from the city of Halle had tested "positive" and was therefore not allowed to travel out of the country. In order to hush up the incident, the team's administration called together athletes from all the various sports and gave them a "very urgent message": Every athlete should "pay close attention and have all necessary papers in order." Otherwise the same thing could happen to them as had happened to their poor athlete-friend from Halle: "That is, he was missing a vital document and therefore not allowed to accompany the team out of the country."

This veiled type of reference was typical. At least the older athletes knew that they were provided with substances that improved their athletic abilities. For us, of course, it was never openly talked about, and no one would ever have admitted such a thing. Consequently, this behavior led to ridiculous situations.

In the Potsdam swimming center, during one specific "cycle" that was considered preparation for the 1987 European Cup final, a strange ceremony took place. Five groups trained together in pools 50 meters long and 15 meters wide. Every group had its own trainer. When every swimmer had finished his/her drill, each trainer unfolded a card table at the edge of the pool. Each group had to line

The Socialist Sports Program

up by their "attendant" to receive their "vitamins"—or so went the official version.

I was responsible for eight female athletes at the time and thus had eight piles of mixed vitamins, iron, and potassium-magnesium on my table. In addition, in my shoulder bag on the floor was a little bottle of Oral-Turinabol tablets. They were not to be placed on the table. The "delivery" followed in the form of a hearty handshake.

One after the other, the swimmers stretched out their hands to me, palms upward. I then gave each of them my right hand and thus distributed the "blues." The girls balled their hands into fists and put their hands to their mouths. On one occasion I had forgotten to press the tablet into Grit Müller's hand. She remained standing at the table for a moment and then said, "Mr. Regner, something is missing."

Indeed, I was able to observe this ritual with every person in the swimming center, but no one ever mentioned a word about it. Also, no coach was to know how much another coach gave to his or her athletes. After all, the effective provision of anabolics for the athletes guaranteed the success, and so the reputation, of each trainer; at this point any collegiality ceased. One time, when I wanted to know from Lutz Wanja what dosage he designated to his athletes, he smiled slightly and said: "You will have to find that out for yourself." A trainer could agree on a dosage only with the team physician.

Thus, Dr. Neubauer had, at the beginning, worked out a framework for my group's plan. According to the plan, the older athletes received the blue 5-mg tablets from the original packaging. For the younger athletes I received an envelope of 1-mg tablets—white, yellow, and sometimes pink.

I adjusted the "distribution" for each cycle according to the course of our training. We called this the "three-and-a-half-day rhythm." For three days the athletes had practice twice a day. On the first two days, I gave each of the swimmers one-half of a tablet, on the third day, a whole tablet. On the fourth day, practice was only in the morning so they did not receive anything.

In such phases all the girls gained, on average, two to five pounds, which could be attributed almost solely to muscle growth. In addition, I realized that the dose I administered to my long-distance swimmers was too high. Heide Grün, for example, became too tight from this; all her muscles tensed up. The dosage was optimal for breaststrokers and backstrokers. Even the younger athletes displayed the desired increase in athletic achievement. Therefore, we repeated this same cycle before the GDR championships in July 1988.

The drug scandal in Seoul concerning Ben Johnson, the Canadian sprinter, threw everyone in GDR sports into a state of panic. The fact that one of the world's best athletes could have been caught had a shocking effect. No one knew whether there was even a future in drug use. Under these circumstances, in November 1988, over a cup of coffee in the staff room next to the swimming center, I brought up the subject with my colleague, Lutz Wanja. In response to my doubts, he replied very brusquely. He argued that everyone was doing it anyway and that "drug use is common everywhere...and if you don't do it, you are pretty stupid."

One month earlier, the head swimming coach of the ASK, Knut Kempa, had given a very surprising order: "Nothing is to happen anymore," he told us. The Sports Medicine Administration was looking for new methods, but Mr. Kempa told us "in the interim, to stop." Later I heard from Dr. Neubauer that during this period new drugs were being tested that were to be taken as nasal spray. However, according to the doctor, this experiment had not yet "proved a success."

Particularly during this awkward phase, my naïveté proved nearly "fatal." For a certain period of time, I had to

The Socialist Sports Program

stay at home in bed with the flu. Knut Kempa had taken over my training group and was looking in my office for my team's training plans. I had lost the key to my desk, so it was unlocked. He was able to search freely through the desk drawers. In the bottom drawer, he found a few Oral-Turinabol foil packages, which I had unwittingly failed to destroy. On my first day back, he called me into his office and reprimanded me: "If this happens one more time, you will be banned from coaching."

The insecurity among sports officials as to when and how drugs should be administered lasted for two months. In January 1989 a meeting of high-level coaches and selected physicians took place at the swimming training center in Lindow. Jürgen Tanneberger, our team trainer, reported that other teams, such as canoe racers, had even gone to Seoul "without an interruption," as he put it. Things were "obviously not as bad" as they had originally seemed. We finally received official orders from the Committee on Sports Medicine to "proceed with work as usual."

I realized that for a long time I had not really been privy to all of the State secrets. The next cycle was scheduled for the period of April 4-13, 1989. It was to prepare the swimmers for the national competition against the Soviet Union in Gera.

During this event Dr. Neubauer disclosed to me that the distribution of Oral-Turinabol was merely the first phase in the perfection of an ultimate preparatory plan. This initial stage was supposedly labeled "M1."* I was then to administer another kind of medication for four days. In professional circles the new drug was referred to as "M2." From April 14 to 17 I gave each female athlete a white 5-mg tablet daily, which I once again received from the doctor in an envelope.

---

*It has since been proven that "M1" was just a new code name for Oral-Turinabol. "M2" was the code for a much stronger androgenic hormone called Mestanolon or "steroid substance 646" (STS 646).

Before the European Championships, to be held in August in Bonn, the cycle had to be repeated twice more, each time at a high-altitude training camp. During such trips out of the country, it was particularly awkward to transport the anabolic steroids.

On May 4, before I set out for the training camp in Zachkadsor, Armenia (USSR), I had to pack a variety of pills in a small opaque bottle labeled with my name. Our team doctor, Horst Tausch, picked it up at the airport. After every coach had turned in his/her medication, Dr. Tausch stowed it away in his medical handbag, which he then sealed. The tablets for my athletes were returned to me only after our arrival in the Soviet Union.

The "M1" cycle was to be carried out from May 7 to 27. During the first week, I quickly determined that the timespan was too long for me. I explained this to my athletes: "Take care, girls, the cycle is too long for my taste. We are here only to prepare for the GDR championships. After all, we don't want to use a cannon to fire at sparrows." The GDR championships began on June 13, which explained why "M2" was to be administered from May 28 to 31. Tablets were not to be taken during the twelve days before a competition. I also renounced "M2" in this instance because I did not want to "overfeed" my athletes.

During these days we coaches often ate supper together in our rooms. We listened to music, and each coach placed tablets on the table in front of him—vitamins, iron, and also the "blues"—which had already been counted out for the following day. Stefan Hetzer was the only colleague with whom I could discuss the subject of drug use.

For instance, he told me that both of his defending champion swimmers, Kristin Otto (who collected six gold medals in Seoul in 1988) and Silke Hörner (who won two gold medals), were to "remain clean" this time as a result of the overriding fear about improved drug screening. Mr. Hetzer also said that both girls would perhaps" not

The Socialist Sports Program

receive anything" for the entire coming year because the more often these drugs were taken, the higher the next dosage would have to be to achieve the desired effect. He told me that only his young competitors would further participate in the cycle.

In Armenia, I experienced firsthand the intense effect that anabolic steroids could have. I underwent what was my second "self-applied experimentation." I "doped" myself in order to be able to judge the consequences. With the second dosage I increased the allotment significantly and took up to ten milligrams daily, which was two tablets of Oral-Turinabol. In addition, I trained as if possessed—I went through two grueling hours of power training a day. The result: A torn muscle in my upper thigh and permanent nightly cramps, which made it necessary for Stefan Hetzer to massage my muscles. Nevertheless, I could tell that I was in incredible physical shape. I gained almost nine pounds of muscle.

Thus, the magnitude of this drug's contribution to GDR sports became crystal clear to me. In general, with corresponding talent and training, anabolic steroids can have an enormously powerful effect. Youths between the ages of fourteen and fifteen can be systematically built up and, in a relatively short time, can achieve a world-class level. Without the drugs, they would hardly attain this level, like a motor that must be "tuned" to function effectively.

If such pills are swallowed irresponsibly, the effect can be deleterious. Apparently, there were coaches in the GDR who still supplied their athletes with an excess of drugs. At the high-altitude training camp in Toluca, Mexico, where preparation for the European Championships in Bonn was held, I was placed in charge of Enja Eichorst, a swimmer from the city of Rostock. Before the flight took off, her hometown coach, Ingold Jopke, explained her "required" dosage to me. The girl was expected to swallow up to ten milligrams of drugs a day, which I considered complete insanity. As a result, during the cycle from July 4 to 31, I gave to her the same amount of drugs I gave my other swimmers.

During this period, for the first time in my coaching career, I thought seriously of leaving the business. On the flight from East Berlin to Mexico, during the stopover in Amsterdam, it occurred to me that I had forgotten to give my medication to the team doctor. I was still carrying the pills in my handbag. I sat down next to Dr. Tausch and asked him what I should do. With an ashen face, he gave me the following advice: "Keep them on your person and be careful how you get through border control." In case of emergency, he told me I was to "declare [the drugs] as heart medication."

For a moment I was determined to stay in Amsterdam. I was frightened and could already imagine the malicious headlines in the Western press. Even if the story never broke, I thought I was finished. I thought that I was no longer sustainable as an accomplice in the secret plan.

However, the border-crossing took place smoothly, and the subject was never brought up again. Dr. Tausch must have kept the incident a secret in order not to compromise his own security. We were dependent on each other.

Although the usual "doping" methods had been happily applied in Toluca, trainers now had to adhere to stricter rules. The head coach, Wolfgang Richter, demanded that everything "that could trigger suspicion about us in any way" was to cease. To begin with, the doctor did not hand out all of the tablets to the coaches at the beginning of the cycle. Instead, these were distributed in three-day rations. In addition, the pills could no longer be distributed in the swimming center. Instead, the athletes went to their coaches at night and picked up their drug quota for the following day.

I shared my first-floor hotel room with a colleague from Magdeburg, Wolfgang Sack, who was coaching the best GDR female swimmers at the time: Kathleen Nord,

The Socialist Sports Program

Olympic champion, World and European champion; Anke Möhring, three-time European champion; and Astrid Strauss, who had won a silver medal at the Olympic games. In the evenings we counted out the tablets and packed them in vials. The athletes then visited us, picked up the vials, and disappeared. One evening one of Wolfgang Sack's swimmers forgot to pick up the tablets. In answer to his inquiry on the following day, she replied guilelessly: "We talked about it among ourselves and we shared, we split it all halfway."

The day eventually arrived when I quite suddenly realized that I could no longer remain true to my career. I knew that I would have to get out of this cesspool. From August 7 to 10, in Chemnitz, named Karl Marx City by the East German leaders, a final training session for the European championships took place. Dr. Tausch took me aside and gave me an order: "Send the girls over to me. They're going to receive a shot in the backside." He told me that I would have to reckon with the fact that "in the ensuing days they could have coordination difficulties." In reply to my inquiry as to what kind of injection they would be receiving, I received a gruff response: "That is none of your business." It had never been so clear to me before that competitive sports in the GDR were organized exactly like the army.

I "fooled" the girls one last time because I did not want to endanger their start in Bonn. I told them that the injections would merely mitigate the effects of the adjustment from the low atmospheric pressure of Mexico to the higher pressure of the lowland level. In Chemnitz, I came to the depressing realization that I had officially been responsible for children and youth for many years, but that at a crucial moment I had to play a merely peripheral role. I had lost ultimate influence over the girls because, in the end, any superior was able to do whatever he wanted to do with them. The State had had the final word.

* * *

Brigitte Berendonk

Author's note: The androgenic hormonal drugs that were systematically applied in GDR sports to athletes of most disciplines, including minors, are known for their damaging side effects. Besides increased muscle tone, tight muscles, and cramps, often resulting in injuries, these include, for example, liver damage and risk of liver tumors, cardiovascular damage due to lowered production of certain blood lipid-binding proteins, heart muscle damage, severe acne, increased aggressiveness, psychotic disorders, and specifically with female athletes, increased libido, genital disorders and malformations such as lack of menstruation (amenorrhea), hypertrophy of the genitalia, multiple ovarian cysts and ovarian inflammations, and unusual body hair growth (hirsutism). The few courageous former GDR swimmers who have publicly described how they were treated with androgenic hormones as minors include Christiane Knacke-Sommer (the first woman to swim the 100 meter butterfly in less than one minute, Olympic bronze medal winner in Moscow 1980), Rica Reinisch (winner of three Olympic gold medals in Moscow) and Raik Hannemann (European Vice-Champion).

Since coach Michael Regner first confessed the criminal truth behind the Olympic successes of GDR swimmers (in the weekly news magazine *Der Spiegel*, March 1990) secret documents of the former GDR government, its Academy of Sciences, and its sports associations have been found that have confirmed his report and have also disclosed the leading persons and the institutions responsible for the barbaric drug research program. These documents include an official *Comprehensive Report 1988* of the "Governmental Plan Theme 14.25," a secret doping research program comprising more than 20 different projects, one of them devoted to the performance enhancement in swimming and gymnastics of 14- to 16-year-old girls. The authors of this report, Drs. Günter Rademacher and Günter Baumgart of the Sports Research

The Socialist Sports Program

Institute (FKS) in the city of Leipzig, are still practicing. Dr. Baumgart is a swimming coach, as is Stefan Hetzer and many other GDR coaches who administered drugs to athletes. Jürgen Tanneberger is now a head coach in the city of Düsseldorf; Dr. Neubauer is still a sports doctor, now employed by the Ministry for Defense of the Federal Republic of Germany. Other GDR swimming coaches are now working in other countries, notably Austria and China. The Chief Medical Officer responsible for the drug research program, Professor Dr. Rüdiger Häcker, has left Germany and is now practicing in Austria. The former Chief Doctor of the Sports Medical Service of the GDR and Member of the Medical Commission of the International Track and Field Federation (JAAF), Dr. Manfred Höppner, who organized the GDR doping program, works as a physician in the city of Berlin. Professor Dr. Edelfried Buggel, former State Secretary in the GDR government and the person ultimately responsible for "Governmental Plan Theme 14.25" research, has recently been elected Honorary Member of the International Society for Sports Science and Nutrition by acclamation.

In the world of sports, politics, and television there is no time for shame. The dope must go on.

Translated from the German by Heidi Whitesell

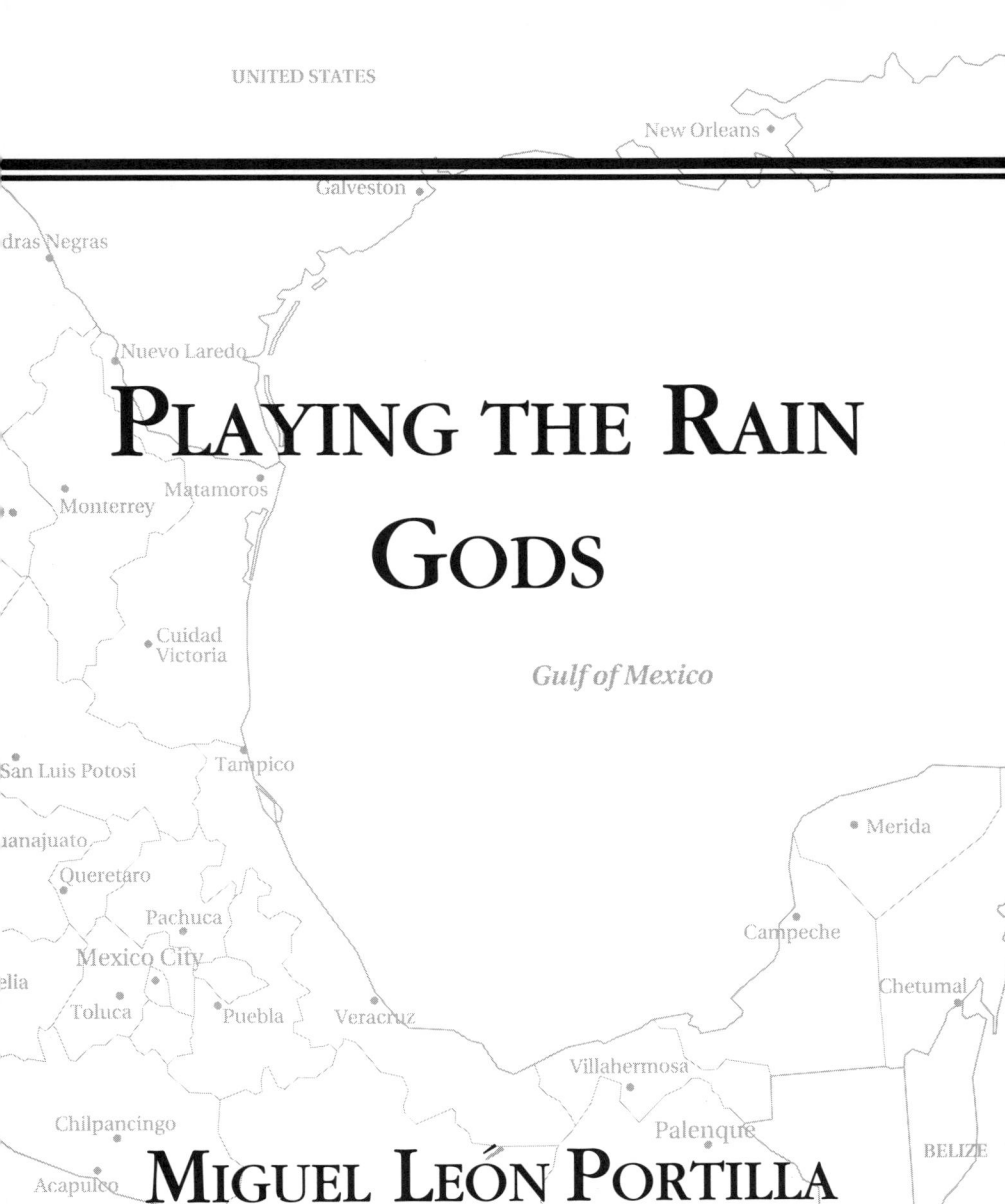

Playing the Rain Gods

Miguel León Portilla

Miguel León Portilla was born 1926 in Mexico City. He is one of Mexico's most accomplished and respected historians. A professor at the National University of Mexico, he is editor of two scholarly journals devoted to the indigenous peoples of Mexico and a frequent guest lecturer at universities around the world.

Professor León Portilla has received various honors both at home and abroad. He was awarded the Elias Sourasky Prize for research in the humanities by the Mexican Secretary of Education in 1966, a Guggenheim Fellowship in 1969, a Fulbright Fellowship in 1976, and Mexico's National Prize in Social Sciences, History, and Philosophy in 1981, among others. He has been the Mexican ambassador to UNESCO, and is a two-term member of the steering committee of the Smithsonian Institution's Quincentenary Commission. He has received four honorary doctorates, in France, Israel, Mexico, and the United States.

Professor León Portilla is the author of twenty-five books and more than one hundred fifty articles.

He is married to historian Ascención Hernández Triviño. They have one daughter.

Playing the Rain Gods

Within the religious worldview of the peoples of pre-Hispanic Mexico, contests—be they between the gods within their divine universe of heavenly bodies, or among men—could take the form of a ballgame. In the ancient books of Mesoamerican paintings and hieroglyphics, we can see how the gods used to play: how the Sun, the Moon, the Morning Star, and other heavenly bodies faced off against each other, the universe their playing field, in a cosmic confrontation between light and darkness.

The sacred areas in the ancient cities of Mexico, what we now call archeological zones, included the ballcourts or *tlachcos* where the Indians had played this ballgame for centuries. These constructions differ greatly. But each *tlachco*, or place for the ballgame, also formed part of the site that made it possible for humans and gods to approach each other. When humans played the ballgame, the confrontation between divine beings was evoked.

This game swelled with meaning for the Mesoamerican people. We know that it was the reenactment of marvelous deeds, a rite, an occasion of competition and betting, a recreation and a joy for the ancient Mexicans. Some descriptive phrases for the game are eloquent in themselves: *Nahualtlachco*, the place of the magical game; *Citlaltlachco*, in the ballgame of the stars; *Teotlachco*, where the gods play ball; *Cuahtlachco*, the ballgame of the rain; and also, of course, simply *tlachco*, where with a ball, humans compete.

Despite their variations, the *tlachcos* have several distinctive architectural characteristics. The court proper is a rectangular courtyard paved with a sort of cement. Smaller perpendicular rectangles, also paved, were at either end, making the shape of a double T. Running the length of either side of the main rectangle were straight walls, or

143

The tlachco *at Chichén-Itzá.*

sometimes walls that sloped inward toward the court, topped with something like a sidewalk. In the middle of the playing field, high on either wall, were carved stone rings through which a ball could pass. In some cases, instead of rings, there were niches at two corners of the walls.

More than fifty *tlachcos* are known from the southern part of the Mayan territory north to the central valley of Mexico and farther still, as at the fortified site of La Quemada in Zacatecas. The *tlachcos* do not always have the same dimensions or even the same proportions. Some are relatively small, others very large, extraordinary artistic monuments such as that at Chichén-Itzá, in Yucatan. Carved images of gods, inscriptions, and other sacred symbols found at such sites indicate that the ballgame was closely related to the religious beliefs and the worldview of the inhabitants.

The totality of meanings inherent in the game are manifold—joy, betting, ritual, and remembrance of primeval events. To begin to comprehend it, one must consider the

The sacred area at Uxmal, with tlachco *at right.*

cultural context of Ancient Mexico.

Ancient texts convey the belief of the Mesoamerican people that the ballgame was taught to humans by the gods, who competed with them. One narrative, the Legend of the Suns, relates that among the events presaging the destruction of Tula, the city of the Toltec wise men, was the appearance of the rain gods. They arrived to invite the supreme human ruler, Huémac, to play ball with them:

And Huémac played the ballgame. He competed against the gods of rain, the *tlaloqueh*. They asked him: "What will we get if we win?" Huémac replied: "My jade, my precious quetzal feathers." The gods of rain told Huémac: "You shall receive the same, our jade, our precious quetzal feathers."

And so they played. Huémac was the victor. The gods of rain then went to get what they had for Huémac, tender ears of corn green as quetzal feathers, and corn leaves green as jade, within which the ears of corn were found.

But Huémac rejected them, saying: "Is this what I get for my triumph? Can these be the jade, the precious quetzal feathers? Take them away!"

The gods of rain then said: "It is all right. Give him the

145

jade and the precious quetzal feathers. Let us take our jade, our precious quetzal feathers: the tender ears of corn and the green leaves that surround them." Immediately, they took them and left, saying: "It is all right, now we will hide our jade, the ears of corn. Now the Toltecs will suffer four years of famine..."*

The consequences of a man's victory in a ballgame in which he opposed no less than the gods of rain were unfortunate.

Chroniclers of the Conquest of Mexico, such as Diego Durán (circa 1536-1588) in his *History of the Indies in New Spain*, and Bernardino de Sahagún (1499-1590) in his *History of the Things in New Spain*, as well as several texts in the Nahuatl language, describe the physical constructs required for this game. Such descriptions can now be compared with the actual archeological discoveries.

Durán offers the following description: "These ball-courts were larger in some places than in others..., narrow in the middle and wide at the ends; there were corners built [at the ends] with the purpose that once the ball went in, the players would not be able to gain any advantage and would commit a foul. The walls were a state or a state-and-a-half in height [approximately seven feet]. Around [the walls], on the outside, they would plant, out of superstition, wild palm trees or red frisol [bean] trees which have soft or light wood...The [tops of the] walls [were crenelated] or had evenly spaced sculpted images all around, and they would be crowded when throngs of people showed up for the games featuring their rulers, [who were] able to play when warfare stopped due to a truce or some other reason.

Chimalpopoca Codex, Primo Velázquez, ed. (Mexico City: Universidad Nacional Autónoma de México, Instituto de Investigaciones Históricas, 1975), p. 126.

Playing the Rain Gods

"These ballcourts were 100 and 150 and 200 feet in length, and those square spaces at the ends of the ballcourt accommodated scores of players who would stand guard, forewarned that the ball should not be allowed to go in; the main players would stand in the middle [of the court], facing the ball and their opponents, for the game resembled their manner of warfare or combat. Affixed to the middle of each side wall were two stones facing each other. Each had a hole in the center...The stone on one side was for [one team, which attempted] to put the ball through the hole that the stone had, and the one on the other side was for the opposing team. Whichever team put the ball through that stone would win the prize..."*

This description is a faithful portrait of the monuments that still stand. It is true that there were differences with regard to the size of the courts. It bears remembering that the old ballcourt erected in Yaxchilán, in the Usumacinta River Basin, is approximately four and a half yards tall and thirty-four in length. The one in Palenque is much smaller. The archeological area in Tula, in turn, has two ballcourts with very different dimensions.

Aside from variations in size, there are other significant differences. The oldest edifices, the ones in the Mayan territory and those of the Zapotec region in Oaxaca, have straight walls. In these types of *tlachcos,* stone rings were placed at the center of each facing side wall. On the other hand, in those courts with sloped inner walls, two niches, placed on opposite corners, substituted for the rings. In the great *tlachco* at Monte Albán, Oaxaca, there is a niche at the southeastern corner and another at the far end of the same wall at the northeastern corner.

Durán provided a description of the players' prepara-

---

*Diego Durán, *History of the Indies of New Spain and Inland Isles*, Angel María Garibay K., ed., 2 vols. (Mexico City: Editorial Porrúa, 1967), vol. II, p. 207.

tions and the attire. "At nightfall, these players would take the ball and place it on a clean platter as well as the leather breeches and gloves used for their protection. They would hang all this from a pole, and, crouched before this playing gear, they would worship it and address it with certain words of superstition and incantation, with great devotion, imploring the ball to be favorable to them [the next] day..."*

Some Nahuatl and various Mayan texts contain a description and name for each piece of equipment. First was the *olli* (rubber) ball. The leather glove was called *mayéhuatl*, or leather of the hand. The hip protector was the *quecéhuatl*, leather of the hip.

The fact that they covered the hip indicates that the ball was hit with that part of the body. As seen in the codices, the *mayéhuatl* protected the hand used by the player to support himself on the ground. It allowed him to hit the ball with greater force. According to Durán's account, the players touched the ball only with their buttocks or knees. It was considered a foul to touch it with any other part of the body.**

Through the ancient Mesoamerican books, we know that the players wore nothing but their breeches and the leather protectors. Sometimes it was a match between pairs, sometimes the number varied. Toribio Motolinía (1495-1569), the Chronicler, who no doubt witnessed some of these competitions shortly after the Conquest, writes:

"They would play two against two, three against three, and sometimes two against three...The lords would bring along great players to play against each other..."

"And after they began to throw the ball around, those who could hit it over the facing wall or hit [the facing] wall with it, would be awarded a line [point]; also if

---

**Ibid.*, vol. II, p. 209.
***Ibid.*, vol. II p. 206.

Playing the Rain Gods

somone hit the opponent [with the ball] or if someone played badly, hitting with part of the body other than the hip, [the opponents] would get a line, and the game would continue until reaching a prearranged total of lines. They would not [stop the ball before it reached the out-of-bounds zones or the place where the receiving players were poised to return it]. Other [players] would [step in to meet the ball]. And the one side would stay within their bounds, as would the other [neither would cross the line that divided the field in half exactly at the point where the stone rings were placed]. Sometimes they would play three against two..."*

Durán explicitly states, "I saw the game played many times." He notes: "...the ball would go from one end to the other for an hour without stopping, without a foul being committed, hitting it solely with the buttocks...the players of one side as well as the other were well aware that they should not stop it, such that it was a thing of wonder..."**

The main rules of the *tlachco* could be thus enumerated:

1. The number of players varied. Each team took its place and played without stepping over the dividing line marked on the ground exactly at the middle of the field, at the point where the stone rings were placed on either side.

2. The ball could be hit only with the buttocks, unless it had been agreed that it could also be hit with the knees, shoulders, or back.

3. The game was played to a predetermined number of lines or points.

4. A line was scored whenever the ball went over the middle line and hit the wall of the opposing team. This fact shows that, in addition to the line across the middle of

---

*Toribio de Benavente Motolinía, *Memories or Book of the Things of New Spain*, Edmundo O'Gorman, ed. (Mexico City: Universidad Nacional Autónoma de México, Instituto de Investigaciones Históricas, 1971), p. 381.

**Durán, *op. cit.*, vol. II, p. 206.

the field, there was another running the length of the field, dividing the *tlachco* in half lengthwise.* Also, evidence of stone markers running the length of the field has been discovered in several *tlachcos*, such as those of Tenam Rosario and Yaxchilán, Chiapas, and Piedras Negras, Guatemala, and others.

5. Hitting an opponent's body with the ball or hitting the ball with other than the hip constituted a foul, which resulted in the opposing team's receiving a line.

6. The game meant continuous volleying back and forth, since the players would not stop the ball before it reached the foul area or the part of the field at either end of the main ballfield where stood the players who had to return it. The game took at least an hour to play.

7. Putting the ball through the hole in the stone ring—a very difficult feat given the narrow space of the hoop—immediately conferred victory on the team that achieved it. The game, nonetheless, could be won without performing such a feat, simply by scoring a given number of lines.

Archeological research reveals that from time immemorial, a form of ballgame similar to that of the Mesoamerican people was known in Brazil's Matto Grosso and its surrounding regions. The similarities are even greater regarding what was called the *batey* game of the Arahuaco Indians of the Carribean.

We know from some of the descriptions of the Chroniclers of the Conquest as much as from archeological discovery, that the natives of several places—such as Haiti, Puerto Rico, Cuba, and other islands—used solid rubber balls, which they hit around with parts of the body other than their hands or feet: the hips, the back, the forearms, and, on occasion, the head as well.

---

*See *Tonalámatl of Aubin*, Carmen Aguilera, ed. (Tlaxcala: Gobierno del Estado, 1983), p. 19.

Playing the Rain Gods

Some scholars have explained the existence of those games as resulting from Mesoamerican cultural expansion. Conversely, others believe that Ancient Mexico's game developed from games that originated in various eastern and northern places of South America and the Caribbean.

In Mesoamerica, the oldest playing fields are found in Mayan lands, which are closest to the Caribbean Islands. They date from the Classical period, in some cases from the first century of the Common Era. *Tlachcos* have been discovered in places like Copán, Honduras; Cobá, Quintana Roo; Yaxchilán and Piedras Negras, in the Usumacinta River Basin at the border with Guatemala; Palenque, in Chiapas; Uxmal, Zayil, and several other sites in Yucatán; Edzná, Calakmul, and several others in Campeche. This may mean that the Mayan region adopted the practice of playing ball as a result of a cultural expansion from the Caribbean.

In the valley of Oaxaca, in a place close to the town named Macuilxochitl in honor of the god of fiestas and ballgames, an archeological site with various carved stones depicting ballplayers was discovered. The exact site is known as Dainzú. The figures appear to be attired in the typical costume of ballplayers. Moreover, one of these figures has a ball in his hand, and wears the arm and knee pads that they used while competing. The Dainzú site dates to around 300 BC. This may mean that the ballgame was played in various places in Ancient Mexico even before the Preclassic Period of Mesoamerica (2500-0 BC).

Either the players or the spectators placed large bets on the ballgames. The mythological wagered game between Huémac and the gods of rain appears to be the antecedent of the practice on earth. Friar Bernardino de Sahagún maintains that, aside from the professional players, the Indian lords and noblemen themselves occasionally participated in these competitions. And Sahagún comments that the lords sometimes ordered that the game be played to uplift his people's spirits.*

Warriors, too, often sought comfort on the ballcourts. For example: Nezahualcóyotl (1402-1472), harassed by his enemies, took a moment away from his worries to play ball.**

The motive was mostly recreation and merriment. Whenever the game was played, however, bets were commonly placed. There were also some primarily interested in this aspect of the game, and the bets might become very large:

"All sorts of valuable things would be lost, precious metal, jade, turquoise, slaves, fine linen, prized breeches, sown lands, houses, leather leggings, bracelets made of precious metal, capes made of duck feathers, loads of cocoa; this was what would be handed over there."***

The common people also engaged in betting. On occasion, their love of the game led them to bet their own bodies. In such cases, they could become slaves or even be sacrificed to the gods.

Durán notes that "a great multitude of lords and gentlemen would attend these games and betting places...And, if a player was able to hit the ball through the stone ring, then it was the custom to present him with all the capes worn by spectators; so that, in the thick of the game, one could hear this occasional shout: Tell thy women to spin their yarn faster, for you will have need for blankets [capes]. On other occasions they would say: Go forth to the market to pur-

---

Florentine Codex (text of the Indian Informants of Sahagún), manuscripts 218-220 of the Palatine collection, Medicea Laurenciana Library, 3 vols., facsimile edition (Mexico City: Government of Mexico, 1979), vol. II, folium 41 v.

**Xolotl Codex*, Charles E. Dibble, ed., 2nd edition (Mexico City: Universidad Nacional Autónoma de México, Instituto de Investigaciones Históricas, 1980).

****Florentine Codex*, vol. II, folium 118 r-v.

chase clothes."*

In light of this, one can better understand Durán's observation that the most cosmopolitan cities and towns built high-walled ballcourts, with handsome and very ornamented walls. Likewise the Aztecs received thousands of rubber balls for their ballgames as tribute from the hinterlands.**

The ballgame of the ancient cultures of Mesoamerica was known not only to those who lived in what became known as New Spain, but also to some who saw it played at the Court of Charles V, in the Iberian Peninsula.

In 1529, Charles V witnessed with his own eyes a ballgame performed in his Court. The previous year, Hernán Cortés had returned to Spain to inform the Emperor of his deeds, to defend himself concerning certain accusations, and to obtain the favors he felt he deserved.

Several notables from Mesoamerica traveled with him. Finding himself in the Court at Toledo, Cortés decided to have some of them demonstrate, for the King's amusement, how they enjoyed themselves by playing ball. It was a fortunate coincidence that the painter Christopher Weiditz, originally from Strasbourg, found himself at this performance. Vividly attracted by the spectacle, Weiditz took several notes, which allowed him to prepare drawings with their respective commentaries, based on what he had been able to observe.

He made 151 drawings, 31 of them in color. In one of them, he included the following note: "These are the Indians that Ferdinand Cortesius brought before His Majesty from the Indies and who, with their wooden implements and ball, have played before His Majesty."***

---

*Durán, *op. cit.*, vol. II, p. 208.
**See *Tribute Register* (Mexico City: Secretaría de Hacienda, 1968).
***Christopher Weiditz's drawings of ballplayers have been reproduced by Howard F. Cline, "Hernán Cortés and the Aztec Indians in Spain" (*The Quarterly Journal of the Library of Congress*, vol. 26, no. 2, April 1969), pp. 70-90.

Another drawing shows two Mesoamericans playing ball with the typical attire. On it, Weiditz wrote: "This is the way in which the Indians play with the inflated ball. With their buttocks, without lifting their hands from the ground; they have a leather protector on their buttocks to receive there the impact of the ball. They wear a kind of leather glove as well."*

Weiditz thus left this early testimony of a game never before seen in Europe. It was his privilege to leave behind visual evidence of an entertainment rich in symbolism. Due to strange circumstances, the ballgame was seen in the Old World only seven years after the Conquest of Mexico.

Remarkably, this ballgame has somehow survived in Mexico through the centuries and up to the present, although the rules have been modified. One can see it played in various villages inhabited by the Cahita Indians in Sinaloa state and among the Mixtecs of Oaxaca state.

The ancient sculptures of ballplayers still in existence evoke the same fascination as was elicited by the ball playing of Cortes's companions who delighted Charles V with their game four and a half centuries ago. We can perceive now what His Majesty did not suspect: In that game, in a veiled manner, the confrontations between divine beings were evoked; in addition, it was a symbol of the cycles of the Morning Star, of Sun and Moon, whose light would shine equally, although at different moments, on the Old and the New Worlds.

Translated from the Spanish by Iván Zatz

---

*Loc. cit.

LA MÁSCARA!
LA MÁSCARA!

ANDREW COE

Andrew Coe was born in Knoxville, Tennessee, in 1959. He studied at Johns Hopkins University and has been a free-lance writer for eight years. Mr. Coe has attended Mexican wrestling matches in almost every major Mexican city as well as abroad in arenas as far away as Chicago and New York.

Mr. Coe is the author of two guidebooks, *Introduction to Mexico* and *Introduction to Mexico City*, to be published by Passport Guides in fall 1992 and spring 1993, respectively. In addition, his work has appeared in the *San Francisco Examiner*, *Popular Mechanics*, and the *New York Daily News*, among other publications.

When not visiting Mexican wrestling arenas, Mr. Coe lives in Hoboken, New Jersey.

La Máscara! La Máscara!

Masked wrestlers stalk each other across a ring in Mexico City. Above, thousands of faces peer down from the upper levels of the arena. Atlantis, in a blue and white mask, is the captain of the *técnico* side. Their evil *rudo* opponents are led by Fuerza Guerrera ("Warrior Force"), who wears a red and black mask with sinister, slanting eyeholes. In round one Atlantis and Fuerza faced off, and Fuerza lost the test of strength. Then Atlantis ducked Fuerza's clothesline and as he passed kicked him in the rump. Fuerza fell on his rear and scooted across the mat in pain, pointing at his behind to the referee in complaint. The audience laughed. The *rudos* grabbed Atlantis's arms and held him against the ropes. Fuerza tried to sock him, Atlantis ducked, and Fuerza knocked his own partners onto the floor. After the *rudos* were pinned to end the round, Fuerza shoved his teammates in exasperation. The audience jeered.

Round two. Atlantis and Fuerza Guerrera circle and clinch. Another test of strength, but this time Fuerza suddenly kicks Atlantis in the shin, doubling him over. The villain is in control. He twists Atlantis's arm and tosses him about the ring, smashing his head into the turnbuckle and encouraging his fellow *rudos* to slug the hero. Fuerza forces Atlantis to the mat with his arms pulled behind him and moaning in pain. "Do something, ref!" the audience shouts. Fuerza grabs the eyeholes of Atlantis's mask and begins to rip. Wrestling magazine photographers crowd around the ring, trying to get the money shot. A portion of the hero's true face is exposed. The audience are on their feet, aghast yet unable to tear their eyes from that patch of his forehead. Atlantis's partners enter the ring to save him but are grabbed by the other *rudos* and pinned. The ref signals the round is over. The arena erupts in catcalls. Fuerza

Guerrera gestures to them, "Come on. I'll take you all on!" The *técnicos* crawl from the ring and rest outside for the final round.

Masks were once common in rural Mexico. On a village's saint's day, peasants donned masks and performed in the dances and parades of the fiesta. The masks represented tigers, goats, donkeys, bats, lizards, deer, birds, serpents, rabbits, caimans, monkeys, and armadillos. These animalistic images were usually vestiges of pre-Hispanic gods. Death and various demons were also popular. Other masks were based on post-Conquest imagery: Moors and Christians, Black Slaves, the Virgin of Guadalupe, and cowboys. Community values and history were taught and reinforced through these dances. They were also a welcome entertainment in the village's poverty-stricken existence. The peasants believed that their identities resided in their faces; when they wore a mask, they hid their true soul and were transformed. They became gods and had the power to convert the brutal world of animal spirits they inhabited into one that was fertile and life-giving.

These traditional ways begin to be forgotten when paved roads arrive at a village, bringing with them urban Mexican culture. The natural world recedes, replaced by the pressing demands of television, newspapers, comic books, and Mexico's intrusive governmental apparatus. Nobody puts on masks at the fiesta anymore, because they have learned that they are already wearing them. The essence of this new life is combat, which in the end they must always lose. Perro Aguayo, one of the great maskless wrestlers, told me: "Why do I need to wear a mask? I'm already wearing one!" Rage, jealousy, treachery, and violence are everywhere, and the only way to endure them is to put on a mask of stoicism and resignation every time they step outside their home. "We are frightened by other people's glances," says Octavio Paz, "because the body

La Máscara! La Máscara!

reveals rather than hides our private selves." If they take off their masks and open themselves up, all that will be revealed is that they are weak, lonely, crying, and mortal.

With the arrival of the greater urban culture, rural villagers learn that they are impoverished. The only option becomes to move to Mexico City in the hope of a better life. In the seventy years since the Mexican revolution, millions have streamed to the capital, leaving women, children, and old people back in their villages. If they are lucky enough to have spare time and spending money, the new city-dwellers divert themselves in cavernous, government-owned movie palaces and enormous sports arenas holding tens of thousands. One of these new entertainments was imported from the United States in 1933 by Salvador Lutteroth, a retired revolutionary army colonel; it is *lucha libre* or "free fighting," the Mexican version of professional wrestling. Through it, real masks—not symbolic ones—have found their way back into Mexican life.

The first *lucha libre* mask was a gimmick. In 1934 an American wrestler brought the leather mask down from Chicago, and Lutteroth liked the idea. He was dubbed El Enmascarado, "The Masked Man," and fought a few matches against other Americans in Mexico City (there were only a handful of Mexican wrestlers at this time). This mask provided the model for all those that have followed: form-fitting and covering the entire head. Two years later the promoter decided to bring back masks. Antonio Martinez, a sporting goods retailer, sewed a leather mask for Cyclone McKay, another American, who became El Maravilla Enmascarado. Soon the Masked Marvel was drawing crowds, and the newspapers were calling him "hated and mysterious"—the mask was a hit. Perhaps a reason for the Masked Marvel's success was that masks were suddenly the rage in Mexico City's popular culture.

The impulse for this craze came from abroad, the United States and France. In 1936 a New York newspaper published the debut of "The Phantom," featuring the first great masked and costumed comic strip vigilante. Also known as The Ghost Who Walks, the Phantom wore a skin-tight purple jumpsuit, striped trunks, and a black mask over his eyes. Unlike most later masked heroes, he almost always wore his mask, even when he was relaxing at home in his skull-shaped cave. In fact, he usually appeared unmasked as a disguise when he was trying to infiltrate some enemy hideout and not tip them off that he was the Phantom. The strip was an instant success and soon sold to newspapers worldwide. Suddenly the Mexican public demanded to see wrestlers in masks, and the promoters realized that they were on to a good thing.

Another popular adventure tale in Mexico City of the 1930s was *The Man in the Iron Mask* by Alexandre Dumas. The title character is Philippe, who is the identical twin brother of Louis XIV of France. The king imprisons his brother in a castle and tortures him until the end of his days by having his head encased in an iron mask that is impossible to remove. When Philippe's true love finds him at the end, the interior of the mask is rusted with his tears. The mask meant pain, and it was unchangeable—that was life in Mexico City. After reading this book, a young wrestler named Rudy Guzmán decided to model his masked character after The Man in the Iron Mask. He became El Santo, El Enmascarado de Plata ("The Saint, The Man in the Silver Mask"), the most famous Mexican wrestler of all time.

Rodolfo Guzmán Huerta moved to Mexico City as a youth and quickly fell in love with *lucha libre*. He trained at the Police Casino gym and in 1939 made his wrestling debut as Rudy Guzmán in one of the city's smaller arenas. He was a *rudo*, the Mexican version of the heel or bad guy, and had some impact on the wrestling world but not enough for his ambition. All his friends were donning masks, so he decided to follow suit. His first adopted persona was Murcielago II (The Bat II); this name was a ploy to catch some of the glory of the original Murcielago, the Mexican champion. Unfortunately, Murcielago objected, and Rudy quickly had to drop the idea. A promoter suggested a new name, El Santo, Rudy added "The Man in the Silver Mask," and a legend was born. Santo's costume was silver, and his mask sported the distinctive teardrop-shaped eyeholes.

El Santo moved quickly to build his name. He switched from the *rudos* camp to the *científicos*, "the babyfaces" or good guys, who were naturally more popular. He cultivated his reputation out of the ring and became known for being polite, generous, honest, and kind to children. And most important: He never removed his mask. When a film crew traveled to Miami for a shoot, Santo flew on a different plane so nobody on the production would see his face when he removed his mask for customs. In his films he even wore his mask when sleeping and when making out with the beautiful female Interpol agents.

Through wrestling, and also films and comic books, Santo became the first Latin American superhero, popular in places as far away as Lebanon. His mask was the equivalent of Superman's "S"—instantly and universally recognizable. Journalists assured fans that despite his fame, when he walked the streets without his mask he blended with the crowd, just a humble member of Mexico City's millions. When he finally retired in the early 1980s, Santo halted his career by publicly unmasking himself. Underneath he *was* humble; bald, with dark bags under his eyes, he looked like a retired factory worker or craftsman. In 1984 he died of a heart attack, and he lay in state once more masked as in life. Other masked wrestlers attended the wake, tears flowing from their eyeholes. The homely Rodolfo Guzmán Huerta hardly existed; the person buried in the Mausoleo del Angel crypt adorned with a silver bust of the masked hero was El Santo.

In the wake of Santo's success, *lucha libre* began to shed its North American characteristics and become more distinctly Mexican. The mania for masks, which few wrestlers wear in the United States, was just one of many changes. The conflict in U.S. professional wrestling is usually defined as a fight between the good "American" wrestler and the wicked, treacherous foreigner. This did not play for very long in Mexico, because the country has not had the same experience of waves of new immigrants arriving and stirring up racist and nativist feelings. In the 1940s, the essential struggle in every *lucha libre* bout was redefined as a battle between *rudo* and *científico*, also known as *técnico*. Santo exemplified the *técnico* side; modest, upstanding, and clean-fighting, he was the pride of the community. The *rudo* was his antithesis. These were the ugly, hairy, and misshapen bullies, mean drunks, and corrupt cops that stalked honest, hardworking citizens and made life hell. *Lucha libre* represented the daily battle on the streets of Mexico City.

As the plot became more Mexican, the characters followed suit. The earliest masked characters were simplistic—Santo's brother donned a black mask and became Black Guzmán—but wrestlers soon realized that they were limited only by the power of their imaginations. Characters began to appear that exemplified the rigors of life in urban Mexico. The white-masked Medico Asesino ("Assassin Doctor") was a doctor in real life, but in the ring he was a *rudo*, because that's how you survive, by being tough and mean.

Another Mexican innovation in the 1940s was the mask-vs.-mask match. The promoters saw that the audience loved the mystery of masks; how better to excite them than with a glimpse of what lay below? The rules are simple: the loser of the bout is stripped of his mask and can never wear one again. His face is exposed to the multitudes, and his real name is published throughout the

La Máscara! La Máscara!

country. The unmasking is a moment of the highest drama; a mythic figure is about to plunge back down to the ranks of the all-too-human. From now on, no matter how threatening and defiant the wrestler is, the audience will always have something on him: his true identity. He is an object of ridicule and humiliation but also of pity. Every Mexico City resident knows that events—from an earthquake to a run-in with a cop—can strip their brave facades in an instant, exposing them, naked and helpless, to the outside world. Wrestlers agree to mask-vs.-mask matches because to lose means a big payday. They can lose their mask only once in a career, so they can demand a year's salary or more for one night's work. The winners are given the mask, and every champion wrestler has a trophy room in which opponents' masks hang on the walls like scalps. Masks are also forcibly removed during regular matches to heat up the fans, but this is technically illegal and these mask losses are never permanent. Promoters rarely schedule mask-vs.-mask matches because of the expense and to avoid overexposure of what for the fan is the ultimate moment of *lucha libre*.

Today nearly every young wrestler starts his career masked. Outside the arenas, masked wrestlers appear at awards ceremonies, wrestling movie premieres, and at demonstrations called by the National Union of Wrestlers and Referees. Child-sized wrestling masks are the most popular gifts on Three Kings Day, when Mexican children receive their holiday presents. The symbol of the Asamblea de Barrios, a grass-roots movement to defend Mexico's poor neighborhoods, is an overweight wrestler named Superbarrio. He leads marches, disrupts the Mexican Congress, and has become a respected national figure of the left-wing opposition. Masked wrestlers are even showing up in the paintings of major avant-garde artists.

Back in the villages, where the craft of mask-making is

all but forgotten, where the best old masks have been sold to collectors, and where only a few old-timers still have the complete costume for the dances, you now see youths joining the fiestas wearing tights, trunks, capes, and the masks of their favorite *lucha libre* heroes.

The announcer blows the whistle to signal the start of round three. Atlantis jumps in the ring with his torn mask and points to Fuerza Guerrera. Fuerza refuses until the audience begins to chant "Scaredy!" and he climbs through the ropes. Hoping to continue with his momentum from round two, Fuerza opens with a blow to Atlantis's mid-section and then puts him in a submission hold. The hero struggles to his feet, slips behind Fuerza, and suddenly has him in the same hold. Quickly Atlantis unties the knot at the back of Fuerza's mask and begins to unlace it. The ref grabs the hero's arms to stop him, because this is against the rules. "*La máscara! La máscara!*" screams the audience. The other *rudos* run in and slug Atlantis, freeing Fuerza from the hold. Using the ropes like slingshots, the wrestlers fly across the ring at each other. The audience knows that Fuerza's mask is held on only by gravity. Atlantis and Fuerza miss contact, but as the *rudo* sails past, Atlantis reaches out and grabs the mask clean off his head. For a second Fuerza's naked face is plain to see by everybody in the arena. His eyes are shut, as if in hiding. Flashbulbs pop, the crowd erupts. Fuerza falls to the mat, covering his face with his hands. Atlantis promenades around the ring with the empty red and black mask held high. The *rudos* are declared the victors by disqualification for the illegal removal of the mask. One of Fuerza's teammates finds a towel, wraps it around his head, and leads him back to the lockers. The *técnicos* stay in the ring a few minutes longer to acknowledge the fans' ovation. The audience file out with smiles on their faces, because for once—no matter what the ref said—things turned out right in this vast, corrupt, and dangerous city.

Glossary

acquiesce—agree or consent without protest, but without enthusiasm
affinity—a close relationship, connection
agnostic—of the belief that the human mind cannot know whether there is a god or an ultimate cause
androgen—any substance that promotes masculine characteristics
androgyne—person having both male and female characteristics
anabolic—having to do with the process by which food is converted into living tissue
archetype—the original pattern, or model, from which all other things of the same kind are made; prototype
arcane—understood by only a few; esoteric
cadre—an operational unit, as of key personnel, around which an expanded organization can be built
corpulence—fatness or stoutness of body; obesity
dour—hard, stern; severe
effervescent—lively and high-spirited
efficacious—having the intended result
effulgence—great brightness; radiance; brilliance
egalitarian—of or advocating or characterized by the belief that all people should have equal rights
empiricism—a method whereby one seeks knowledge by observation and experiment
existential—concerning a modern philosophical movement encompassing several themes, among them that the universe is absurd and irrational, and emphasizing the phenomena of human anxiety and alienation
fetid—having a bad smell, as of decay; stinking; putrid
germane—truly relevant; pertinent; to the point
hegemony—dominance, especially that of the state or nation over others
homogeneous—composed of similar or identical elements or parts; uniform

Glossary

hypertrophy—a considerable increase in the size of an organ or tissue
laconic—brief or terse in speech or expression
malapropism—ludicrous misuse of words
metaphysical—beyond the physical or material; supernatural
myopic—nearsighted
narcissistic—evidencing excessive interest in oneself
paradigm—a pattern, example, or model
pervade—to be prevalent throughout
rampant—spreading unchecked; widespread; rife
repository—a person or thing thought of as a center or accumulation of storage
repudiate—to refuse to have anything to do with; disown or cast off publicly
rescind—to revoke, repeal, or cancel
sacrosanct—very sacred, holy, or inviolable
secularize—to deprive of religious significance
segue—an immediate transition from one point to another
stoicism—studied indifference to pleasure or pain
subversive—tending or seeking to overthrow or destroy
tandem—a relationship involving cooperative action
utilitarianism—the ethical doctrine that the purpose of all action should be to bring about the greatest happiness for the greatest number
veritable—being such truly or in fact; actual
warble—to make a musical sound; babble as a stream

Bibliography

Adair, Robert K. *The Physics of Baseball*. New York: Perennial Library, 1990. Nonfiction: The questions and quirks of baseball explained through physics.

Angell, Roger. *Late Innings: A Baseball Companion*. New York: Ballantine Books, 1983. Nonfiction: A compilation of essays (1977-1981), originally written for *The New Yorker*.

Angell, Roger. *Season Ticket: A Baseball Companion*. New York: Ballantine Books, 1989. Nonfiction: A collection of essays from 1982 through the 1986 World Series.

Ashe, Arthur, Jr. *A Hard Road to Glory*. New York: Warner Books, 1988. Nonfiction: A comprehensive history of African Americans in sports from the 17th century to the present.

Bondy, Filip, and Araton, Harvey. *The Selling of the Green: The Financial Rise and Moral Decline of the Boston Celtics*. New York: Harper Collins, 1992. Nonfiction: Interviewing more than 100 sources, two sportswriters tell us how the Celtics' wheels of power turn.

Bryan, Mike. *Baseball Lives*. New York: Pantheon, 1988. Nonfiction: Men and women of the game talk about their jobs, their lives, and the national pastime.

Dargan, Amanda, and Zeitlan, Steven. *City Play*. New Brunswick: Rutgers University Press, 1990. Nonfiction: Text and photographs explore the urban games children play in New York.

Deford, Frank. *The World's Tallest Midget*. Boston: Little, Brown, 1987. Nonfiction: A collection of articles originally written for *Sports Illustrated*.

Gregorich, Barbara. *She's on First*. Chicago: Contemporary Books, 1987. Fiction: The story of one of the first women in professional baseball.

Guttman, Allen. *A Whole New Ball Game: An Interpretation of Sports*. Chapel Hill: University of North Carolina Press, 1988. Nonfiction: A social history showing how American sports reflect American culture.

Bibliography

James, C. L. R. *Beyond a Boundary.* New York: Pantheon, 1984. Nonfiction: James explores the classlessness that the cricket pitch allowed in the class-bound world of the post-colonial Caribbean.

Krich, John. *El Beisbol.* New York: Prentice-Hall Press, 1989. Nonfiction: A witty look at baseball in Latin America.

Mangan, James A. *Sport in Africa.* New York: Africana Publishing Company, 1987. Nonfiction: A collection of original essays exploring the social, political, and ethical dimensions of African sport.

McCrone, Kathleen E. *Playing the Game: Sport and the Physical Emancipation of English Women.* Lexington: University Press of Kentucky, 1988. Nonfiction: A comprehensive, humorous overview of every aspect of women in sports.

Norbent, Elias, and Dunning, Eric. *Quest for Excitement: Sport and Leisure in the Civilizing Process.* Cambridge: Blackwell Publishers, 1986. Nonfiction: A review of sports in several societies, from Classical Greek wrestling to the British gentleman's fox hunt.

Oxendine, Joseph B. *American Indian Sports Heritage.* Champaign, IL: Human Kinetics Books, 1988. Nonfiction: A description of the emphasis on sports and games in the traditional life of Native Americans.

Ramsey, Russell W., and Khromov, Yuri G. *Ten Soviet Sports Stars.* Boston: Brandon Books, 1992. Nonfiction: Written by a TASS reporter and an American colonel, this book takes an objective look at Soviet sports.

Sanson, David. *Greek Athletics and the Genesis of Sport.* Berkeley: University of California Press, 1988. Nonfiction: A search for the definition of sport and how it is related to ancient civilizations.

Sheed, Wilfred. *Baseball and Lesser Sports.* New York: Harper Collins, 1991. Nonfiction: An autobiographical story of a boy emigrating from England to the US, exchanging cricket for baseball, British culture for American.

Index

A
Andalusia, 113-122
Arahuaco Indians, 150
Aztecs, 62, 153

B
ballgame, 70, 143-154
Baltimore Colts, 41-49
baseball, 41-49, 69
Baumgart, Günter, 138-139
Beijing, 77-91
belts, sumo, 26, 29
Block, Diana, 123, 125, 127
Brazil, 71
bullfighting, 113-122
bulls, breeding of, 115-116

C
Charles V, 153-154
Chicago Cubs, 41-49
China, Goodwill tour of, 77-94
class system, Japanese, 20-21
coach
    football, 77-91
    GDR sports, 123-139
competition, sumo, 20, 28, 30-33
corrida, 121-123
Cortés, Hernán, 153-154
culture
    American, 54-55
    Andalusian, 113-122
    Mexican, 159
    reflected in sports, 70, 73

D
deities
    ancient, 53
    heavenly, 71
Diem, Carl, 70-71
Domecq y Díez, Alvaro, 115
drugs, performance-enhancing, 123-139
    testing for, 129-130
Durán, Diego, 146, 147-148, 149, 152

E
Eichorst, Enja, 135-136
Elia, Lee, 45-46
European Cup, 127, 130, 134
Evangel College football team, 77-91

F
fans, sport, 41-49
Felshin, Jan, 58

football, 57, 64, 69
    American tour of China, 77-94
fans, 48
Forbidden City, 77, 85
franchises, sport, 43-49
Frederickson, Florence S., 53, 55, 63
Frobenius, Leo, 53, 66

G
gambling
    on lice racing, 101-107
    on Mesoamerican ballgame, 144, 151-152
games, 62
    of earth and sky, 71
    rules of, 65-66, 149-150
German Democratic Republic (GDR), 123-139
godhood, sumo, 28-29
gods, 68
    pre-Hispanic, 144, 158
    rain, 143, 145, 151
    warrior, Japanese, 19
governing body, sumo, 27, 30, 36-38
Gronau, Katrin, 127
Grün, Heide, 127
Guttman, Allen, 70, 72, 73
Guzmán Huerta, Rudolfo, 160-161

H
Hart, Marie, 59
Hawaiian, 23, 38, 63
hero-villain (*técnico/rudo*), 157-164
Hoefner, Jürgen, 128
horses, training for bullfighting, 117-118
Hörner, Silke, 134
Hetzer, Stefan, 134, 135, 139
Huémac, 145-146, 151
Huizinga, Johan, 59-62, 66, 72-73

I
injuries, sport, 3-15
Ireland, 3-15
Irsay, Robert, 43-44
Isaac, Barbara, 68-69

J
Japan, 19-38
    baseball teams in, 47
    journalist, 49-49, 88

K
Kempa, Knut, 132-133
Knacke-Sommer, Christine, 138

169

Index

L
lucha libre, 159-164
lice racing, 97-107
Li Peng, 79-91
loyalty, team, 41-49
Lukas, Gerhard, 69-70
Lutteroth, Salvador, 159

M
Man in the Iron Mask, The, 160
Mao Zedong, 77-94
master-apprentice system, Japanese, 23, 24-25
Mayan territory, 144, 147, 151
McIntosh, Peter C., 64, 66
Mesoamerica, 143-154
Mestanolon, 133-134
Mexico, 143-154, 157-164
Meyer, Corinna, 127
Möhring, Anke, 137
Motolinía, Toribio, 148
Müller, Grit, 123, 125, 127, 131
mythology, 57, 72

N
names, as element in sumo, 22, 33-35
Neubauer, Jochen, 124, 127, 131, 139
Nord, Kathleen, 126
Northrop, F. S. C., 60

O
Olympic Games, 54, 79, 102, 127, 137, 138
Pacific Lutheran University football team, 77-91
Papua New Guinea, 63-64, 71
play, as basis of culture, 58-62, 65-67
playing field, 66-67
    football, 90-91
    Mesoamerican ballgame, 143-154
Pound, Ezra, 57
prison, Turkish, 97-107

R
racism, in sumo, 36-37
Rademacher, Günter, 138-139
Regner, Michael, 123-139
rejoneador, 113-122
relay race, 71
religion, as root of sports, 21, 53, 56, 67, 72-74
ring, purification of, 21-22
ritual, in sports, 21, 53-74, 143-154
running, 70
    cross-country, 3-15
    for exercise, 81-82

S
Sack, Wolfgang, 136-137
Sahagún, Bernardino de, 146, 151
samurai wrestlers, 20-21
Schmitz, Kenneth L., 60, 61, 62
Spain, 113-122
sport, national
    American, 41-49
    Japanese, 19-38
sports
    early American, 55
    Marxist view of, 70
    system, GDR, 123-139
Sports Medicine, Committee on, 129-130, 133
stable, sumo, 21
steroid, androgenic-anabolic, 125-139
Strauss, Astrid, 137
sumo, 19-38
sun/moon rituals, 66, 71, 143
swimmers, 123-139

T
Tanneberger, Jürgen, 133, 139
Tausch, Horst, 134, 136, 137
television, sport coverage, 46-49
Toltec Indians, 145
topknot, sumo, 21, 26, 32
torero, 113-122
tourism, Spanish, 118-120
Tribune Company, 44-49
Turkey, 97-107
typhus, epidemic of, 100

W
Wanja, Lutz, 128, 131, 132
war, 64-65
    games, 57-58, 64, 71
    weapons, 64-65
    stone, 68-69
Weiditz, Christopher, 153-154
Westering, Frosty, 83-91
Wood, J. G., 69
wrestlers, 19-38
    masked, 157-164
wrestling, 70
    mask-vs.-mask, 163-164
    societal role of, 63
Wrigley, Phil, 44

Z
Zietermann, Franziska, 127

WITHDRAWN
No longer the property of the
Boston Public Library.
Sale of this material benefits the Library.